TEMPLE
WORSHIP
Simplified

TEMPLE
WORSHIP
Simplified

TERRANCE DRAKE

CFI
Springville, Utah

ISBN 13: 978-1-59955-332-0

Published by CFI, an imprint of Cedar Fort, Inc., 2373 W. 700 S., Springville, UT 84663
Distributed by Cedar Fort, Inc., www.cedarfort.com

LIBRARY OF CONGRESS CATALOGING-IN-PUBLICATION DATA

Drake, Terrance S.
  Temple worship simplified / Terrance S. Drake.
     p. cm.
  ISBN 978-1-59955-332-0
  1. Mormon temples. 2. Temple endowments (Mormon Church) 3. Temple work (Mormon Church) I. Title.

  BX8643.T4D73 2009
  264'.093--dc22

  2009032031

Cover design by Megan Whittier
Cover design © 2009 by Lyle Mortimer
Edited and typeset by Melissa J. Caldwell

Printed in the United States of America

10 9 8 7 6 5 4 3 2 1

Printed on acid-free paper

Dedicated to Marvia Lynn,
my eternal sweetheart

Contents

Introduction

There are 151 temples announced, in construction, or in operation at the writing of this book. It has been estimated that with the completion of all the announced temples, over 80 percent of the membership of the Church will be within a two to three hour drive of a temple. There will be many more in the future. President Brigham Young gave this vision of temple construction in these latter days, "To accomplish this work there will have to be not only one temple but thousands of them, and thousands and tens of thousands of men and women will go into those temples and officiate for people who have lived as far back as the Lord shall reveal."[1]

For many, temple service remains something unique and somewhat mysterious. It is generally understood that all aspects of temple ordinances are important and that the temple is a sacred and holy place where a special feeling of peace and reverence is present. It is also understood that we never speak of the sacred ordinances of the temple in any detail beyond the walls of that sacred building. Beyond these common understandings there are, however, many questions that remain unanswered for the majority of those who come to the temple: What is the full significance of the recommend? Why do we receive the same narrative every time, word for word? Can we learn from such repetition and if so, how? Why the lack of formal teaching? Why the absence of questions and answers? What if I fall asleep during the session? What is the difference between working in the temple and worshipping in the temple? Does the veil ever part and are these sacred events recorded? Have apostates revealed the truths of the temple on the Internet, and if so, what does this have to do with me? Is there knowledge about the temple that is withheld from the general membership?

My purpose in writing this book is to answer these types of questions without intruding to any degree into those sacred areas that must only be discussed in the temple itself. The answers to these questions should broaden our perspective of temple activity and enhance our ability to approach and serve within the temple with greater understanding and appreciation for this special component of our personal worship of God.

It has been a complete joy writing about the temple. This book could properly be viewed as a "temple primer" wherein I have presented insight that I have gained over the many years of serving and being served in the house of the Lord. An insight will be introduced with a temple experience and question to ponder at the beginning of each chapter. While serving as an ordinance worker, a sealer, a recorder, and a member of a temple presidency, I have had many special experiences. The information presented in this book has been shared, in part, at stake conferences, sacrament meetings, and priesthood leadership meetings over several years.

All of us attend the temple with certain perceptions, expectations, and uncertainties. The principle perception held by those who attend the temple is that no other activity within the Church has greater eternal significance than the work of the temple. The principle expectation is that we can gain blessings from the temple that are available nowhere else. And the principle uncertainty is that we may not understand or appreciate adequately all the personal growth and truth gained from regular temple attendance. *Temple Worship Simplified* will focus on this area of uncertainty by adding a broader foundation of understanding of temple work, temple worship, and temple policy. This understanding will bless your activity in the house of the Lord whether you have had years of experience within the temple or you are in the earliest phases of temple activity. As these questions are discussed and answered, I hope that you will have an increased desire to attend the temple.

NOTES

1. *Discourses of Brigham Young*, ed. John A. Widtsoe (Salt Lake City: Deseret Book, 1954), 394.

Chapter One

THE RECOMMEND

I t had been a great day. I loved stake temple days, and this one had been particularly successful. The West Stake had turned out in good numbers, and our little temple had been humming since 6:30 A.M. It was now 9:30 P.M., and I was scanning in the final ordinance cards from the last session when Brother Stubbs came into the office. He was one of our most faithful ordinance workers from the East Stake and had been very busy all afternoon.

"It's been a great day, President! How did we do?" he asked enthusiastically.

"We did amazing," I told him. "I don't believe we've ever completed more endowments in a single day."

He stared at me for a minute, and I could tell something was on his mind. I stopped what I was doing and looked at him.

In a much more serious tone, he said, "President, we could have days like this all year long if people were just required to use their recommends. Do you have any idea how many people renew their recommends every two years and almost never come to the temple? You know the old saying, 'Use it or lose it.' I just don't understand how someone can have a recommend and not come to the temple."

His words hung in the air for a minute. I was not quite ready to respond to his comments. It then was obvious that he was not expecting an answer from me as he held out his hand and gave me a firm *handshake. He offered, "Sorry, president, sometimes I get a little carried away. It sure has been a wonderful day."*

"That is has!" I replied. "Thanks for your great work."

QUESTION TO PONDER:

If the temple recommend is so important that it is a necessary prerequisite to qualify a presiding officer in the Church to serve, shouldn't that leader be required to use it? For that matter, why aren't we all required to use our recommends?

Sacred Callings

In late winter 2002, my wife and I were serving in the Dominican Republic as a full-time missionary couple. I was the Area Medical Advisor for the missions of the Caribbean, and my wife served as my assistant. We were also serving as ordinance workers in the Santo Domingo Temple. We received a phone call from the secretary to President James E. Faust of the First Presidency. She arranged a time for us to be together to take a call from President Faust. As we waited for the phone to ring at the designated time, we had a pretty good idea what the phone call would be about—to be called to preside over a mission somewhere in the world. Earlier we had had an interview with one of the Seventy and had been advised that this call might be forthcoming.

When the phone finally rang, we quickly answered it. Our heads were close together so that we could both listen over the one phone we had in our small apartment. President Faust began the interview with one question, "Do you and your wife both hold current temple recommends?"

I answered that we did, and a wonderful interview continued. President Faust extended the call for us to serve in South America.

We returned from our mission in July 2004. We began to settle in again after having been gone for three years from our home and ward. We both received calls to serve in our ward and immediately became temple workers in the Reno Nevada Temple. In October, I received a call from F. Burton Howard of the Seventy, who stated that he was calling on behalf of President Hinckley. He said that before he began the interview he needed to ask me one question: "Do you and your wife both hold current temple recommends?"

Like before, I answered that we did. The interview then continued, and he extended a call for me to serve as first counselor and recorder of the Reno Nevada Temple and for my wife to serve as assistant to the matron of the temple.

I believe it is very significant that both of these calls, extended by the Lord's anointed, began with the very same question: "Do you have a current temple recommend?" Once this question was answered in the affirmative, the interview continued with a mutual confidence and shared understanding that was instantly established between the officer extending the call and individual receiving the call, even though these individuals had not met personally before the conversation. The temple recommend is much more than a simple document that authorizes us to enter the temple.

Symbol of Righteousness

President Hunter taught the principle that members should have a current temple recommend at all times, even when there is little chance that they will attend the temple: "Truly, the Lord desires that His people be a temple-motivated people. It would be the deepest desire of my heart to have every member of the Church be temple worthy. I would hope that every adult member would be worthy of—and carry—a current temple recommend, even if proximity to a temple does not allow immediate or frequent use of it."[1]

President Gordon B. Hinckley also taught of the importance of having a temple recommend, even when one cannot attend the temple with regularity: "Perhaps you cannot get to the temple very often. But even if you cannot get to the temple, I would like to suggest that you go to your bishops and get a temple recommend and carry it with you and regard it as a precious and true thing. It is a credit card, if you please, with the Lord."[2]

Some positions in the Church require a recommend in order to serve. The two personal experiences shared above are examples of this. No man could preside over a mission without being temple worthy. No bishop or stake president could serve if he was not worthy to have a current temple recommend. No man could serve as a common judge with the authority to ask others about their worthiness to enter the temple if he is not worthy himself of a recommend. He would be released immediately if anything in his life became so disordered that he was no longer worthy to have a recommend.

It is important to understand that the recommend does much more than just authorize entry into the temple. It is a symbol of personal commitment to live covenants and to serve God. President Hinckley continues,

> I would hope that every Latter-day Saint who is old enough would have a temple recommend. It says something. It is a priceless, priceless thing to have a temple recommend. It says that we are faithful, that we are doing what we ought to be doing, that we are living the gospel, that we are sustaining our authorities, that we are observing the Word of Wisdom, that we are paying our tithing, that we are treating our families properly, that we are treating our neighbors properly, that we are the kind of people we ought to be.[3]

We need this expanded vision of the recommend or we may be at risk of treating sacred things lightly, as illustrated by the following experience recorded by a bishop over twenty years ago.

> I had known Charles for many years. Our boys attended the same scout troop and we had gone together on many campouts. We had also gone together with the youth of the ward on many temple trips and had enjoyed serving together as we baptized and confirmed in the house of the Lord.
>
> After some years of serving together, I was called as bishop of the ward. We needed a new elders quorum president and my first thoughts were to call Charles. These feelings were made known to the bishopric in a meeting. Soon, thereafter, the financial secretary came to me and advised me that Charles rarely paid his tithing. He

thought I needed to know this before I recommended his name as the new elders quorum president. I was surprised with this information and asked the secretary how this was possible, since I had been with Charles in the temple on many occasions over the past few years.

The secretary explained that Charles would pay his tithing for one to two months before his recommend needed renewing. In this way he continued to have a recommend without paying a full tithing for the rest of the year. I reviewed the records for myself from the previous couple of years and determined that what my finance secretary had shared with me about my friend was true.

After much prayer and meditation over the matter, I called Charles into the office for an interview. I showed him the information from the past two years. It clearly demonstrated that he had paid his tithing only a few times prior to the renewal of his recommend. He was very repentant and admitted that he had failed to pay his tithing for most of each year, but that he was committed to correct this going forward. I felt he was sincere, and I reminded him that his oldest son was turning nineteen in four months and was submitting his papers to serve a mission. I also pointed out to him that he would need to renew his recommend before his son left on his mission, and that I could not sign his recommend if he was not faithful in the law of tithing over the months that remained.

The months passed quickly and the mission papers were sent and the call to serve was received by his son. I was aware that no tithing had been paid by Charles since our interview and assumed that he had decided not to go to the temple with his son. One month or so prior to his son entering the mission field Charles paid a modest sum of tithing. Two more small checks were paid over the next couple of weeks. The following week Charles came to the office to renew his recommend so that he could be with his son in the temple. I dreaded this interview and was praying for some divine direction on how to manage this most difficult situation. I knew that no one but myself and the financial clerk were aware of this problem and that many members of the ward would be going to the temple on that special day to be with this great young man and his father and mother, as he received his endowment and prepared to serve the Lord.

I could see the anguish on his face as he entered the office. I was impressed not to immediately start with a prayer. I asked what he wanted me to do. He looked down and as he stared at his shoes he said, "Please renew my recommend. I want to be with my son in the temple."

I loved this man. We had been friends for years, our wives were friends and our children had grown up together. At first I had no idea how to respond. In my heart I was praying to the Lord to help me know what to do. This was certainly a moment of truth in the life of this father and friend. As I looked into his begging eyes and felt his near panic at the thought of not being with his son in the temple, I wanted to sign the recommend and release him from the pain he was feeling. Two scriptures entered my mind:

"Trifle not with sacred things" (D&C 6:12) and, "Do not ask for that which ye ought not" (D&C 8:10).

At the very moment, when I may have done the wrong thing, the Holy Spirit blessed me with clear understanding of what I should do.

First, I shared my testimony that I knew his son's call to serve a mission had come from God through a living prophet. I promised Charles that this missionary service would bless his son's life, forever. Then I said to him, "We are going to kneel together and pray. I am going to ask you to voice the prayer. When you are through praying, I will do whatever you ask me to do with respect to renewing your recommend. If you say 'Renew it,' I will. All that I ask is that you open your heart to the Lord as we kneel together."

He sat for a minute considering what I had just said. I saw a brief glimmer of hope in his eyes as he and I knelt before the Lord. At first no words came. Then he started his prayer, but the Spirit soon overwhelmed him, and he began to cry. I could not understand all that he was trying to say in the prayer. The sobs were so powerful and racked his body so violently that the real communion was between him and the Lord, and I became nothing more than an observer as he opened his heart to heaven. When the prayer ended, we faced each other. His face was red and streaked with tears. "You cannot renew my recommend!" he blurted with great conviction. "I am not worthy."

Then he continued, "I only ask one thing. You take my place with my son when he enters the temple".

A week later, I emerged from the temple with his wife and his oldest and recently endowed son. Charles was waiting for us. When his son saw his father, he broke into a run. Their embrace was long and sweet. What they whispered to each other none of us could hear, but their love for each other and the joy they were experiencing in that moment touched all of our hearts forever. Soon his wife joined them and there was added joy that cannot be explained or understood except through the Holy Spirit.

The temple recommend symbolizes our obedience, our love of God, and our constancy in striving to live sacred covenants. It is not something we temporarily qualify for so that we can be present for some special family or ward event. When Charles opened his heart to the Lord, he did not need a bishop to tell him that he should not enter the temple.

The recommend is much more than paper to authorize entry into the temple. It is physical evidence that we are striving month after month and year after year to live this life according to the will of God.

Free to Choose

The question asked at the beginning of this chapter, however, that has thus far been left unanswered is this: The recommend is important, both as a symbol of faithfulness and a document authorizing entry into the temple of God, but are we required to use it? If I am a stake president or a bishop, I must have a recommend to serve, but is someone going to check up on me to be sure I am attending the temple? Is there written somewhere a minimum number of times I must attend the temple? Is someone keeping a record of attendance? Will someone come to my office and advise me that I cannot continue to serve unless I go to the temple more often? I will be released if I fail to have a recommend, but will I be released if I never use it? The answer to all of these questions is simply no.

Much has been said about the importance of attending the temple. There is almost always some reference to the importance of regular temple attendance in each general conference. There have been many special instructions and words of encouragement for members to go to the temple as often as they can. Great blessings and greater understanding of sacred things have been promised to those who attend the temple. To understand why temple attendance is completely a "free-will" offering, consider the following statement by President Gordon B. Hinckley:

> I hope that everyone gets to the temple on a regular basis. I hope your children over twelve years of age have the opportunity of going to the temple to be baptized for the dead. If we are a temple-going people, we will be a better people, we will be better fathers and husbands, we will be better wives and mothers. I know your lives are busy. I know that you have much to do. But I make you a promise that if you will go to the House of the Lord, you will be blessed; life will be better for you. Now, please, please, my beloved brethren and sisters, avail yourselves of the great opportunity to go to the Lord's house and thereby partake of all of the marvelous blessings that are yours to be received there.[4]

On another occasion, President Hinckley said it like this: "That which goes on in the House of the Lord, . . . comes nearer the spirit of the sacrifice of the Lord than any other activity of which I know. Why? Because it is done by those who give freely of time and substance to do for others that which they cannot do for themselves, and for which they who perform this service expect no thanks or recompense."[5]

Note that the prophet expresses hope that everyone gets to go to the temple on a regular basis. He states his understanding that people's lives are busy and that they have much to do. He promises blessings and then says, "Please, please . . . avail yourselves of the great opportunity to go to the Lord's house." He further states that the work is done by those "who give freely of time." He does not suggest that the members of the Church are obligated to go to the temple. There is no order or command. There is, however, a prophetic invitation, a promise, and a pleading. President Hinckley continues: "Without the spirit of dedication, without the spirit of sacrifice, without the spirit of consecration, temples could not function. That goes without saying. The work in the temple is essential; it is a work of personal sacrifice and individual consecration. There is nothing to compare in all the world."[6]

The key words from this declaration are *dedication, sacrifice,* and *consecration.* These sacred words speak of a higher order of service within the kingdom of God that extends beyond what is commanded or obligated.

President Hinckley has also said the following: "I know of no other work to compare with it. It more nearly approaches the vicarious sacrifice of the Son of God in behalf of all mankind than any other work of which I am aware. Thanks are not expected from those who in the world beyond become the beneficiaries of this consecrated service. It is a service of the living in behalf of the dead. It is a service which is of the very essence of selflessness."[7]

It starts to become clear why there is no requirement, commandment, nor obligation to go and do the work of the temple. President Hinckley's statement that temple work "more nearly approaches the vicarious sacrifice of the Son of God in behalf of all mankind than any other work of which I am aware" elevates temple service above any other activity in the Church. Our choice to go to the temple, this very act of unobligated, unaudited, and often unrecognized service, in a quantitatively small but symbolically rich way, follows the pattern of the Savior. The Savior taught that He freely gave his life: "I lay down my life, that I might take it again. No man taketh it from me, but I lay it down of myself. I have power to lay it down, and I have power to take it again" (John 10:17–18).

He walked the path to Golgotha of his own free will. No man forced him or obligated him to do it. In a rich and symbolically similar way, we likewise go to the temple of our own free will. It is not required of us, it is not commanded of us, and we are completely free to make the choice to serve the dead, or not.

The pattern continues even beyond this principle. Christ gave his perfect body and shed his perfect blood on our behalf. We—in a symbolically similar way—allow our imperfect, mortal bodies to be used to bless the lives of the disembodied spirits as we stand and speak for them in the holy temple. Through the Savior's infinite atoning sacrifice, He did for us what we could never do for ourselves. We, through the offering of temple service, do for others what they cannot do for themselves. Everything about the sacred service in the temple speaks of dedication, sacrifice, and service, just as President Hinckley taught.

Why are members of the Church not forced or obligated to give this service? The spirit of sacrifice and of consecration would be lost. Temple service will always remain outside the circle of those activities we are obligated to do in our callings within the kingdom of God. Temple service must be selfless. It must be freely offered, and it must be given joyfully; only then will our actions begin to be patterned after the perfect example set by the Savior. The greatest promised blessings of mortality are linked to the sacred ordinances of the temple because, in President Hinckley's words, this sacred work "more nearly approaches the vicarious sacrifice of the Son of God in behalf of all mankind than any other work of which I am aware."

NOTES

1. Howard W. Hunter, "First Presidency Message: The Great Symbol of our Membership," *Ensign*, Oct. 1994/

2. Gordon B. Hinckley, *Teachings of Gordon B. Hinckley* (Salt Lake City: Deseret Book, 1997), 631–32.

3. Ibid.

4. Ibid., 624.

5. Ibid., 623

6. Ibid., 640.

Chapter Two

STAYING AWAKE

H e was a big man, about 6'2", and he was in a hurry. He skipped steps as he approached the temple door.

"I'm late!" he blurted out.

I assured him he did not have to worry. "We're a small temple. The session won't start without you."

He smiled gratefully as he entered the locker room that is located outside the recommend desk. He chose to change his clothes there since he was in work clothes. In an amazingly short time he emerged from the locker room, dressed in white, with his recommend ready.

"I'm sorry you had to wait for me."

I assured him it was no problem and that we were happy to have him with us for the afternoon session.

As he entered the session, he took his seat on the second row. There were a number of sisters in attendance, but very few men, as was usually the case for this particular session.

Brother Crane, the ordinance worker who was officiating, gave a smile of greeting to the new arrival and pushed the button to start the session. The familiar words of greeting began instantly. Soon the lights began to dim and as the room became dark, the eyes of the big man sitting in row two became very heavy, and for the next forty-five minutes, he nodded in and out of consciousness as sleep claimed his attention.

Brother Crane had a big smile on his face as he came down the hall with the ordinance cards to be scanned from the afternoon session.

"How was the session?" I asked

"Great! It went very well, but that last fellow who came in just before the session started sure had trouble staying awake. I sometimes wonder if it does any good to come to the temple if you're just going to sleep through the session. Maybe it would be better to stay home and take a nap."

His question hung in the air for a second or two.

"I saw him as he left the temple. He thanked me again for holding the session. He looked happy for having been here," I offered.

Brother Crane shrugged his shoulders and with a big smile said, "Well, it was a great session. I hope he got something out of it."

QUESTION TO PONDER:

Should you come to the temple if you find it difficult to stay awake and focus on the ordinance?

This chapter will consider the theme of "temple work." For the purposes of this book, temple work is defined as the vicarious performance of the temple ordinances required for each child of God to enter his kingdom and the family history research needed to submit and clear a name for these temple ordinances.

Vicarious Temple Work

In the example above, Brother Crane was concerned as he reflected on the session. He imagined an ideal where each patron would be mentally engaged and alert during the session. Under these circumstances, the patron is blessed as he or she contemplates the rich symbolism of the endowment, and an alert patron would assure that the ordinance was completed correctly and fully. It should be understood, however, that the part of temple work that relates to the performance and recording of vicarious ordinances has nothing to do with the alertness of the patron. Consider all the good that was accomplished in that afternoon session.

1. A sacred ordinance was performed and recorded.

On that afternoon, a working man rushed to make a late afternoon session. He was grateful to participate in the session, and appreciated the temple workers holding the session for a few minutes. He did the work for a person with whom he had no relationship, receiving a name from the general temple inventory. He lost his battle with sleep during the first half of the session. Brother Crane made sure that our patron did all that was required of him during the session. An ordinance had been completed and recorded as the patron, expressing gratitude, excused himself from the temple about an hour and fifty minutes after entering.

Sacred temple work was accomplished. The name of a deceased man had been submitted previous to this particular event as the result of extraction or family research. Another man in mortality had left his worldly occupation to come to the temple and had completed an ordinance on behalf of that deceased individual. Our part in this plan of mercy was completed. Whether this ordinance will be sealed by the Holy Spirit of Promise in heaven cannot be determined by any man on earth. President Gordon B. Hinckley speaks of this process of standing "in behalf of the dead."

> But there are uncounted millions who have walked the earth and who have never had the opportunity to hear the gospel. Shall they be denied such blessings as are offered in the temples of the Church?
>
> Through living proxies who stand in behalf of the dead, the same ordinances are available to those who have passed from mortality. In the spirit world they then are free to accept or reject those earthly ordinances performed for them, including baptism, marriage, and the sealing of family relationships. There must be no compulsion in the work of the Lord, but there must be opportunity.[1]

The opportunity was given for a post-mortal son of God to receive an ordinance essential for exaltation. This was accomplished, and there is nothing in this declaration that suggests that the living proxy must be alert, attentive, and completely focused on each word of the ordinance for this work to stand as valid. A man came to the temple of his own choice and did for another that which he could not do for himself. The temple patron missed some of the narrative of the endowment due to sleepiness, but this did not invalidate the temple work being completed.

2. He came to the temple.

Obviously, sacrifice was involved since this patron arrived alone, in a hurry, and in his work clothes. Sacrifice—for temple work, or any other aspect of the gospel—is a divine attribute. He came to the temple unannounced, neither expecting nor receiving any special recognition for the sacred work he would accomplish. His very act of being in the temple and leaving his work early, matches perfectly with President Hinckley's words given at a Logan Temple Workers Devotional on August 25, 1996: "Without the spirit of dedication, without the spirit of sacrifice, without the spirit of consecration, temples could not function. That goes without saying. The work in the temple is essential; it is a work of personal sacrifice and individual consecration."[2]

Could anyone question this man's dedication, his sacrifice, or his level of consecration? He should feel welcomed and should be treated with love and appreciation as he enters the house of the Lord. His personal battle with sleep is not relevant to accomplishing the vicarious work in the temple. He accomplished all that was necessary to complete the ordinance. His presence alone in the temple blessed his life, blessed the session he attended, and blessed a son of God on the other side of the veil.

3. He may have been touched by the Holy Spirit.

The rich symbolic teaching during a temple session is not limited to the narrative at the beginning. When the lights are down, many struggle to stay awake. It is possible that his heart was touched with additional light and truth during the later part of the session. He may have felt blessings of peace and comfort as he sat in the holy rooms of the temple. Some of the sweetest moments of personal reflection in the temple occur after the session is completed, while one sits in that ever-exquisite room that represents the presence of God.

He may have been strengthened or blessed by the words of the sacred prayer offered during the temple session. His own heartfelt prayers may have been answered and his soul strengthened during the later part of the session when he was engaged and alert. Sometimes one begins a session fighting fatigue, but then there is a word, a gesture, an observation, or a feeling that enters the heart, offering peace or greater understanding, and thus blessing our presence in the temple. An average endowment session in the temple can last anywhere from eighty to ninety minutes depending on the number of patrons. Sleepiness during the first forty-five minutes does not mean that spiritual blessings are negated during the second half of the ordinance when the lights are up and the personal involvement of the patron becomes more active.

4. There may be many other personal blessings gained from this temple visit.

He may have gone home that afternoon after giving selfless service in the temple and been a better father or husband, which is a promised blessing of the temple as taught by President Hunter: "Much work remains to be done, and we continue to encourage you to attend the temple as often as is feasible. Stronger marriages, more attentive parents, and more faithful children will come as a result of following this counsel."[3]

He may have been reminded of his own temple covenants and felt a renewed desire to live them more fully. He may have taught a future lesson with a greater portion of the Holy Spirit. He may have directed his ward, his quorum, his group, or his stake with greater love and patience as a result of his service in the temple. One cannot know all the blessings that are poured out upon God's children when they participate in these sacred ordinances in behalf of others. Elder John A. Widtsoe speaks of the personal help available to each of us as we labor in the temple:

> These are trying days, in which Satan rages, at home and abroad, hard days, evil and ugly days. We stand helpless as it seems before them. We need help. We need strength. We need guidance. Perhaps if we would do our work in behalf of those of the unseen world who

hunger and pray for the work we can do for them, the unseen world would in return give us help in the day of our urgent need. There are more in that other world than there are here. There is more power and strength there than we have here upon this earth. We have but a trifle, and that trifle is taken from the immeasurable power of God. We shall make no mistake in becoming collaborators in the Lord's mighty work for human redemption.[4]

No one can measure all the good that resulted from the visit of this wonderful patron. No one can know the mighty help from the unseen world that he may have received that day, as he became a collaborator in "the Lord's mighty work for human redemption." There should be no concern or comment over his personal wakefulness. Many, if not all, who have attended the temple for any significant period, have struggled with staying completely awake and spiritually engaged during the entire session. Regardless of the level of mental alertness or the level of physical or emotional fatigue of a patron, sacred and exalting ordinances were performed, fulfilling promises made by those of us in mortality to our ancestors, even before the earth was formed. It is holy work. Those who serve in this great work deserve nothing but gratitude, love, kindness, and our highest respect for the selfless service they give, whether their eyes are opened or closed.

Family History Research

As mentioned earlier in this chapter, another key part of temple work is family history. Every ward has individuals who have caught the spirit of family history and have seen miracles in their lives as they sought after their kindred dead. To move forward, the work of the temple depends on this research. Countless individuals, in and out of the Church, have been touched by the Spirit of Elijah and have felt their hearts turn to their fathers, grandfathers, and on back as far as their research will carry them. Family history, and the sacred work in the temple that follows, was part of the Lord's plan from the very beginning and is required as the earth prepares for the second coming of the Savior. In President Joseph F. Smith's vision recorded as section 138 of the Doctrine and Covenants, we read about this eternal doctrine: "The Prophet Elijah was to plant in the hearts of the children the promises made to their fathers. Foreshadowing the great work to be done in the temple of the Lord in the dispensation of the fullness of times, for the redemption of the dead, and the sealing of the children to their parents, lest the whole earth should be smitten with a curse and utterly wasted at this coming" (vv. 47–48).

Promises were made by children to their fathers. We, the living, are the "children" and our kindred dead are the "fathers." When we find our deceased ancestors and do their work, we are fulfilling a promise we made before the foundation of the earth.

Not everyone will be engaged in family history. In fact, it is fair to say that few members of a typical ward are active in researching their ancestors. This group is expected to grow in numbers with the ease and convenience of new family search tools. Nevertheless, excessive zeal in promoting the merits of family history research can send an unintended message as illustrated in the following example:

I had just started serving in the temple presidency and was delighted when Brother Lane invited me to attend a special meeting to see how we could increase temple attendance in our ward. At the meeting were a member of the bishopric, Brother Lane, two of our ward family history consultants, and myself. The meeting went well—Brother Lane proposed a program where family cards would be handed out to members with the challenge that they commit to go to the temple and complete the work during the next two weeks. He was willing to coordinate the distribution of the cards, and the two family history consultants assured us that there were enough family cards held by the two or three most active researchers in our ward, to keep us busy for a very long time. It seemed like a perfect program. The families providing the cards would see the temple work for their ancestors completed more quickly; individuals who might not have otherwise gone to the temple would now go to complete the work they had committed to do; and the ward would be blessed with increased temple attendance.

We then shifted our attention to the issue of how to help members become trained in doing their own genealogic research. Sister Arnold, one of the ward's most outstanding family history consultants, took the lead. She said, "Members will be blessed if they take their own names to the temple. I have found in my own life that if I am not going to the temple for one of my own family members, I hardly enjoy the session. When I know about the person for whom I am serving, I have a rich and spiritual experience. Members need to understand that their temple experience will be made richer and sweeter if they take their own names. For me, if I do not take my own family names, it is hardly worth going."

Her words were sincere and I doubt that anyone, except me, felt uneasy with what she had just said. As the meeting ended I approached Sister Arnold and asked her how many members of our ward were actively engaged in family history research. Her answer did not surprise me. She said that there was only a handful—maybe six or eight—who were trained and took it seriously. I then asked her if there were not scores of members that could benefit from attending the temple. She agreed immediately. I then pointed out to her that she was considered by most members of the ward to be the true expert in family history. She did not disagree with that assessment. Then I asked what I might feel if I were a busy father of a young family, trying to do all that was asked of me, and in that context, heard the family history leader in our ward state that for her, it was not worth going to the temple if she did not take one of her own family names. I asked her if there were not blessings to be obtained by attending the temple, even if we had never engaged in family history research. I watch as she considered what I had said and what I had asked. She immediately understood the point I was making. "President," she said, "I will never share that feeling again when talking to others about going to the temple or about doing their temple work."

We then had a lively discussion where we both recalled earlier seasons in our lives when we had been blessed by regular temple attendance, but had not yet become active in seeking out our dead through family history research.

Family history is a vital part of the temple and brings great blessings as we keep the eternal promises made to our ancestors before the foundation of the world, but family history is not a requirement to go to the temple to receive the great prophetic blessings that have been promised.

President Hinckley promises these blessings to all who may be stressed or troubled with difficult decisions: "The temple is also a place of personal inspiration and revelation. Legion are those who in times of stress, when difficult decisions must be made and perplexing problems must be handled, have come to the temple in a spirit of fasting and prayer to seek divine direction. Many have testified that while voices of revelation were not heard, impressions concerning a course to follow were experienced at that time or later which became answers to their prayer."[5]

These promises are not conditional on the individual taking a personal family name to the temple. Everyone is invited to the temple. For those who have brought family names as the result of their own research, they will surely feel a special spirit. The many who, for whatever reason, are not actively involved in researching their kindred dead still qualify for answers to prayers and the promises of "sacred impressions" as a result of their temple service. All who qualify to enter the temple will face "times of stress" and "difficult decisions." The promised blessing of "divine direction" has nothing to do with whether a patron has a personal family ordinance card in his hand as he enters the temple. It should never be suggested or implied by those who serve or by those who are served in the temple that the most favored temple patrons are those who can stay awake and those who bring their own family names. All are invited to come and all will be blessed.

NOTES

1. Gordon B. Hinckley, "Why These Temples?" *Ensign*, Aug. 1974, 39–40.

2. Hinckley, *Teachings of Gordon B. Hinckley*, 640.

3. Howard W. Hunter, *The Teachings of Howard W. Hunter*, ed. Clyde J. Williams (Salt Lake City: Deseret Book, 1997), 241.

4. John A. Widtsoe, "The Way of Salvation," *Improvement Era*, May 1943, 278–79.

5. Gordon B. Hinckley, "The Salt Lake Temple," *Ensign*, Mar. 1993, 6.

Chapter Three

Silent Learning

The couple stood holding hands and staring through the etched glass doors of the baptistry. The last session of the day had begun and there were no baptisms being performed. The room was empty. Inside was the font with the beautiful chandelier centered over it. The water was completely still, a perfect blue; the picture of the Savior being baptized by John was hanging off to the right. The glass enclosure allowed easy viewing of the oxen that supported the font. They stared in silence.

Brother Bair noticed the couple. He had been an ordinance worker since the temple opened.

"It's beautiful, isn't it?" His words broke their silence. "Come on in so you can get a better look. No one will mind."

Brother Bair swung open the door to the baptistry and ushered the couple in. He immediately began to tell them about his own role in helping to seat the font on the oxen.

"It was a real tough job," he said. "I think our whole high council was here that day. We are very proud of our temple."

Brother Bair then explained his understanding of what the oxen represented and why the font had to be set at the lowest point in the temple. The couple listened as he instructed.

After a few minutes, the couple mentioned that they needed to leave, but they thanked him for his kindness in showing them the baptistry and for all the information he had shared with them.

QUESTION TO PONDER:

Was this couple learning more in their silent observance than they learned from Brother Bair's enthusiastic instruction? How do we learn in the temple?

Much of what is to be learned in the temple will come through silent observation and personal meditation. In this example, a couple was silently considering the grandeur and majesty of the baptistry, while viewing it through closed glass doors. No one can know the thoughts in their hearts and minds as they considered the beauty that lay before them. They were not verbally communicating with each other, yet they were sharing a moment of reverent reflection. Their thoughts may have been personal, perhaps recalling a special family baptism or the sweet memories of ward temple trips from years past. Their thoughts may have been doctrinal, focusing on some aspect of the amazing and merciful plan that allows all men and women to have the same chance to accept or reject the ordinances and blessings of the gospel. Their thoughts may have been operational, wondering, for example, how much water is needed to fill the font, what temperature the water is kept at, or how a small temple could manage so many wet clothes in such a small area.

It is possible, however, that their thoughts were lifted above the normal cognitive processes of remembering, observing, or analyzing; that through the very act of seeing and meditating over that holy place, they were receiving divine light and knowledge so sweet, so pure, so calming and comforting, that no words can describe what they were experiencing. This divine learning, through enlightened eyes and quickened minds, is the way the Lord often communicates his sacred truths to his children without being encumbered by words. It is by his Holy Spirit that we are enlightened with truth that exceeds what the natural man could ever see or understand. It is by this same Spirit that our eyes are opened to the things of God. Consider the following as recorded by the Prophet Joseph Smith in Doctrine and Covenants section 76:

> For by my Spirit will I enlighten them, and by my power will I make known unto them the secrets of my will—yea, even those things which eye has not seen, nor ear heard, nor yet entered into the heart of man.
>
> By the power of the Spirit our eyes were opened and our understandings were enlightened, so as to see and understand the things of God—(vv. 10–11).

Joseph declares the method by which the sacred teaching contained in this great vision was to occur. He states that by the Spirit "our eyes were opened and our understandings were enlightened."

The key for learning then was dependent on something they would see. Through this process of beholding with eyes that were opened spiritually and by understanding that was quickened, they could then see and understand the things of God. The steps were to look first and then, through the process of looking, gain increased and enlightened understanding.

When our eyes are opened to the divine, light or truth enters our souls. We know that there is something wonderful and sacred about what we are seeing and feeling, but the experience is often beyond words. In fact, if the couple from the case presented above tried to explain why they stood in silent contemplation of that sacred room, whatever effort they made to do so would have immediately lessened the sacred quality of their experience; or, even worse, might have completely misrepresented what was occurring in their hearts and minds.

When Brother Bair broke the silence and invited the couple on a tour of the baptistry, his words, although well-intended, instantly terminated any chance of further light and truth being seen or felt through the Spirit. Any knowledge he might have regarding the position of the font in the temple or the significance of the oxen pales in comparison to the majestic light and truth that may have been touching the hearts of this couple as they stood in silent and reverent contemplation.

Man's words have very little use in the temple. The narrative is beautiful and symbolic, and essential ordinances require specific language, but extra words of explanation, clarification, correction, or direction are not necessary. Let the temple speak for itself through the Holy Spirit. A perfect example of how man's words are completely inadequate in explaining or describing sacred and holy things is found in the book of Moses:

> And it came to pass that Moses looked, and beheld the world upon which he was created; and Moses beheld the world and the ends thereof, and all the children of men which are, and which were created; of the same he greatly marveled and wondered.
>
> And the presence of God withdrew from Moses, that his glory was not upon Moses; and Moses was left unto himself. And as he was left unto himself, he fell unto the earth.
>
> And it came to pass that it was for the space of many hours before Moses did again receive his natural strength like unto man; and he said unto himself: Now, for this cause I know that man is nothing, which thing I never had supposed (Moses 1:8–10).

Moses had just beheld the full majesty and glory of God, "the world and the ends there of." Then in that very moment when God withdrew his presence and he "was left unto himself," Left with only words to describe the glorious and magnificent works of God, Moses proclaimed: "Now, for this cause I know that man is nothing, which thing I never had supposed."

Clearly, this was not the principle message that the Lord had intended for Moses in laying before him this great vision. In this same chapter the Lord later declares, "For behold, this is my work and my glory—to bring to pass the immortality and eternal life of man" (Moses 1:39). Moses's statement that "man is nothing" seems, therefore, inaccurate. Man is the object of God's work and glory. Why then did Moses respond as he did? The answer is that words could not even begin to describe adequately the glory of God. Moses understood that what he had just experienced in this vision surpassed any possibility of being able to describe it with any number of words in any language. He gave us, therefore, his best expression of what he felt at that moment, "man is nothing." The context of this rather extreme statement might look something like this: Man is nothing compared to that which my eyes have just beheld.

Divine instruction, accomplished without words, is explained further in the Doctrine and Covenants,

> And the light which shineth, which giveth you light, is through him who enlighteneth your eyes, which is the same light that quickeneth your understandings;
> Which light proceedeth forth from the presence of God to fill the immensity of space (D&C 88:11–12).

This light that proceeds from the presence of God, enlightening eyes and quickening understanding, refers directly to the process of silent learning that was cut short by the well-meaning but overly helpful ordinance worker in the previous example. It is important to understand that we retain a certain responsibility to prepare ourselves so that this type of divine learning can take place. The Lord explains this later in the same section, "And if your eye be single to my glory, your whole bodies shall be filled with light, and there shall be no darkness in you; and that body which is filled with light comprehendeth all things" (D&C 88:67).

Here the Lord qualifies this great promise that our bodies shall be filled with light and that there shall be no darkness in us with this qualification, "If your eye be single to my glory." Revelation through the process of silent meditation will be proportional to our degree of personal righteousness. The prophet Moroni reminds all men that there are conditions for knowing something by the spirit: prayer, a sincere heart, real intent, faith centered in Christ. Then follows the promise that we can know all things:

> And when ye shall receive these things, I would exhort you that ye would ask God, the Eternal Father, in the name of Christ, if these things are not true; and if ye shall ask with a sincere heart, with real intent, having faith in Christ, he will manifest the truth of it unto you, by the power of the Holy Ghost.
> And by the power of the Holy Ghost ye may know the truth of all things. (Moroni 10:4–5)

There is a standard of righteousness assumed when one has qualified to enter the temple. Individual preparation, through obedience and sincere desire, with faith in Christ, will qualify anyone to be taught through this process of silent learning. We can leave the temple refreshed and enlightened without having heard a single extra phrase or comment during our temple experience. We can go week after week and the miracle of this learning never ceases.

This experience of learning and feeling divine things through silent observing is not limited to those with temple recommends or even to those baptized into the Church as illustrated by the following:

Soon after the temple was opened, a few residents that lived near the temple began to complain about the temple lighting that was maintained through the night. The City Council considered their complaint and set a date for members of the community to come and voice their opinions for or against keeping the temple lights on at night. The Mormon community turned out in huge numbers on the night of the hearing. The opposition did not show up to offer their objections.

Even though the legal matter was resolved quickly, the City Council did invite several members of the community to voice their opinions. Various prominent members of the LDS community offered positive statements about the lighting. Some engineering data was shared that showed that the amount of light from the temple was far less than the bright lights of the downtown area. Finally, a lady, who was not a member of the Church, offered these words: "I am not a Mormon and I have no idea what they do in that temple. But I know this, when I have had a bad day or am stressed to my limit, I drive up there at night and sit in my car and look at that building and it brings me peace. It is what a house of God should look like."

This nonmember friend of the Church found peace and received comfort from doing nothing more than silently contemplating the beauty of the temple. Man—regardless of his level of sophistication and learning, regardless of his vast experience in Church service, and regardless of any office he may hold—is incapable of putting adequate words to that which is holy. In section 76 of the Doctrine and Covenants, speaking of the great vision that had just unfolded, we read:

Neither is man capable to make them known, for they are only to be seen and understood by the power of the Holy Spirit, which God bestows on those who love him, and purify themselves before him. (D&C 76:116)

The formula for temple learning is to see and to understand by the power of the Holy Spirit, which God bestows, based on our love for Him and our personal efforts to follow his commandments.

Chapter Four

FINDING ANSWERS

I was in the office reviewing some temple data when Brother Dow came to the door.

"Do you have a minute, President?" He questioned.

I invited him in with a firm handshake.

He introduced himself and told me he had just had an amazing "ah-ha" in the session. He then began to describe in great detail a part of the temple narrative. He said, "I believe this means . . ." and went on to give a most amazing and insightful analysis of what he had felt and what he had learned.

When he was finished with what was a very detailed report on his learning experience, he waited for me to comment.

I looked at him and said, "What you've just shared with me is wonderful. Thank you."

He kept staring, and I could see he wasn't totally satisfied with my response.

Finally, he could not contain himself and blurted out, "But is it right? Did I get it right?"

"I think what you experienced is exactly what the Lord hopes for all of us in the temple," was my only answer.

He then got a wry smile on his face and said, "You're not going to tell me, are you? I know that we are supposed to learn for ourselves in the temple, but when we get it right, shouldn't someone validate what we've learned?"

I assured him that I believed he had added greatly to his own understanding of the endowment and thanked him again for sharing his experience with me. As he left, I could tell he was still not completely satisfied with my response. I had the impression that he believed there was a sacred and carefully guarded book that had all the right answers about the temple and that for some reason I was forbidden to share this knowledge with him.

QUESTION TO PONDER:

How do you know if your understanding of the temple is correct? Is there an authoritative source where all temple truth is outlined, all symbols revealed, and all interpretation provided?

A simple answer to the second part of the question above is that there never has been nor will there ever be an authoritative book that contains all the temple symbols and all the knowledge that can be gained through these symbols. The following statement by President Harold B. Lee explains why this would be impossible:

> These revelations, which are reserved for and taught only to the faithful Church members in sacred temples, constitute what are called the "mysteries of Godliness." The Lord said He had given to Joseph "the keys of the mysteries, and the revelations which are sealed" (D&C 28:7).
>
> To the faithful, the Lord promised: "And to them will I reveal all mysteries, yea, all the hidden mysteries of my kingdom from days of old. . . ." (D&C 76:7).[1]

All the Mysteries of Heaven

The ordinances of the temple offer a way for man, in the Lord's words, to understand "all mysteries, yea, all the hidden mysteries of my kingdom" (D&C 76:7). No individual, regardless of his high office, or years of temple service will ever understand all the truth and all the mysteries that are contained within the rich symbolism of the temple. You could attend the temple daily for your entire adult life and learn something new every day and still not come to know all the "mysteries of Godliness." Elder Boyd K. Packer teaches this principle clearly,

> Have you ever wondered why it is that many patrons of the temple can go session after session, week after week, month after month, year after year, and never become bored or tired or resistant?
>
> How, then, could they continue to learn? The answer to that lies in the fact that the teaching in the temple is symbolic. As we grow and mature and learn from all of the experiences in life, the truths demonstrated in the temple in symbolic fashion take on a renewed meaning. The veil is drawn back a little bit more. Our knowledge and vision of the eternities expands. It is always refreshing.[2]

Elder Packer states that it is "always refreshing." *Always* is the key word.

There will never be a moment, even after long and faithful temple activity, in which an individual could exclaim, "There, I finally know it all!"

The temple ordinances will always have something more to teach about the mysteries of godliness. The notion that somewhere, someone in mortality has all the knowledge of the temple recorded, and that for some chosen individuals this information is available, is just not true. The temple will always allow for greater learning as one attends with a heart that is seeking to learn. But what of the other part of the question posed by Brother Dow? How can we know if we "have got it right"? How can we be sure our understanding is correct?

Learning from Symbols

As one comes to the temple and begins the process of learning from the many narrative and visual symbols that are presented, two facts should be recognized. The first principle of learning from temple symbols is that each symbol will bring us to Christ. Through these symbols we will come to understand the plan of salvation and the need for an atoning sacrifice. They will teach us of our relationship to Christ and to a living Father in Heaven. They will bring to our minds an increased understanding of the absolute truths that include the Creation, the Fall, the Atonement, agency, opposition, a probationary state, judgment, divine promises, and the Savior's central role in all of these. As mentioned previously, the symbolism of the temple contains all the "mysteries of Godliness." We can never exhaust the available learning in one short lifetime of temple attendance.

The second principle of learning through symbols is that each temple symbol represents many levels of truth. As a person returns often to the temple, and at the same time grows in life's experiences through work, service, or personal trials, the same symbol may bring new and deeper understanding. What may have been considered an incidental or insignificant part of the familiar narrative, can, with an enlightened view born out of life's experiences, suddenly teach about divine truths and relationships that were not initially appreciated. Again, in Elder Packer's words, "It is always refreshing."

To illustrate the different layers of meaning available through the same symbol, consider the one symbol from the temple that we can discuss outside the temple. This is baptism by immersion. Baptism is performed for the living as well as the dead, and there is no restriction on discussing this sacred ordinance. It is a richly symbolic ordinance in which the person to be baptized is completely submerged in water. If any part of the clothing or person is not submerged completely, the ordinance must be repeated.

Remembering the two important points regarding learning through symbols—that all temple symbols will bring us to Christ and that there are many levels of understanding—consider the following example of how, hypothetically, a person might progress in his understanding of baptism by immersion over the course of life.

If you asked of a seven-year-old who was preparing for his own baptism, "Why will you be baptized by having your entire body immersed in water?" his answer might sound something like this:

"My body has to be completely put under water so that all my sins are washed away. Every part of me must be made clean."

Although there is obviously some doctrinal problem with the idea that a recently turned eight-year-old has sins to be washed away, this answer, nevertheless, would be acceptable and age-appropriate. The symbol of using water as a cleansing agent and the need for a complete washing is clearly understood by this seven-year-old.

If you asked this young man at age fifteen, "Why were you baptized by immersion eight years ago?" his answer might sound like this: "I was baptized by immersion because that was the way Jesus was baptized by John, and I want to follow His example."

This young man has come to understand how the Savior was baptized by John, perhaps through seminary, family home evening, or Sunday school. He wants to follow the Savior. Implied in what he says is that this will be his pattern for life, following the Savior, not only in baptism by immersion but also in all things.

Now this hypothetical young man reaches age twenty-two and you ask again, "Why were you baptized by immersion fourteen years ago?" His answer: "My baptism by immersion is a symbol of the death and resurrection of Christ. I symbolically die with Christ as I am put under the water, and symbolically resurrect with Christ when I come out of the water."

This represents a mature understanding of the symbol of immersion as taught by Paul in Romans.

> Know ye not, that so many of us as were baptized into Jesus Christ were baptized into his death?
> Therefore we are buried with him by baptism into death: that like as Christ was raised up from the dead by the glory of the Father, even so we also should walk in newness of life.
> For if we have been planted together in the likeness of his death, we shall be also in the likeness of his resurrection. (Romans 6: 3-5)

Being placed completely under water is incompatible with life and is, therefore, a rich symbol of dying. Coming out of the water beautifully represents Christ's victory over death. This young twenty-two-year-old has made the connection between baptism by immersion and the atoning sacrifice and Resurrection of the Savior of the world.

Assume that at age thirty you ask the same question again, "Why were you baptized by immersion so many years ago?" The answer might look like this, "My baptism by immersion is a symbol of being born again. Just as a baby must emerge from a sack of water at the time of birth, symbolically I came out of the water into a 'newness of life' in Christ."

A greater understanding of the symbolism of immersion is evident in this response. This is the very imagery the Savior used as he taught Nicodemus as recorded in the gospel of John.

> There was a man of the Pharisees, named Nicodemus, a ruler of the Jews:
>
> The same came to Jesus by night, and said unto him, Rabbi, we know that thou art a teacher come from God: for no man can do these miracles that thou doest, except God be with him.
>
> Jesus answered and said unto him, Verily, verily, I say unto thee, Except a man be born again, he cannot see the kingdom of God.
>
> Nicodemus saith unto him, how can a man be born when he is old? Can he enter the second time into his mother's womb, and be born?
>
> Jesus answered, Verily, verily, I say unto thee, except a man be born of water and of the Spirit, he cannot enter into the kingdom of God. (John 3:1–5)

True discipleship will require a "mighty change" and the reference to being born again presents a visual image of a complete personal renewal. Alma the Younger speaks of this rebirth and mighty change as he questions the brethren of the Church about their own discipleship:

> And now behold, I ask of you, my brethren of the church, have ye spiritually been born of God? Have ye received his image in your countenances? Have ye experienced this mighty change in your hearts? (Alma 5:14).

The symbol of a rebirth to a newness of life as one comes out of a complete immersion in water is rich and meaningful.

Again, suppose you ask the question of our hypothetical man who has now reached the age of forty, "Why were you baptized by immersion those many years ago?" His response might sound like this, "Baptism by immersion symbolizes all of those concepts I have come to understand and previously shared: being washed of sin, following Christ's example, symbolically dying and resurrecting with the Savior, and being born again. All are important to my understanding, but now I also know that without the baptism of fire, baptism by immersion alone accomplishes nothing. It is through the baptism of fire and the Holy Ghost that I can receive a remission of my sins."

This response adds even more understanding to the symbol of baptism by immersion. It teaches that immersion in the water is important, but the baptism of fire, through the gift of the Holy Ghost is an essential component of this ordinance as recorded in 2 Nephi.

> Wherefore, do the things which I have told you I have seen that your Lord and your Redeemer should do; for, for this cause have they been shown unto me, that ye might know the gate by which ye should enter. For the gate by which ye should enter is repentance and baptism by water; and then cometh a remission of your sins by fire and by the Holy Ghost. (2 Nephi 31:17)

The response of this forty-year-old man demonstrates an understanding of the symbolism of baptism by immersion and the necessary connection between baptism by immersion in water followed by baptism by fire, which is the Holy Ghost. His understanding of the symbolic ordinance has matured with a personal vision of the role of the Holy Ghost in completing the ordinance. Focusing only on the baptism of water is inadequate at his current level of understanding. This essential link is taught clearly by the Prophet Joseph Smith, "You might as well baptize a bag of sand as a man, if not done in view of the remission of sins and getting of the Holy Ghost. Baptism by water is but half a baptism, and is good for nothing without the other half—that is, the baptism of the Holy Ghost."[3]

In this hypothetical presentation, it is evident that at each level of understanding, the symbol taught greater truth about Christ. The seven-year-old clearly recognized the significance of total immersion in water as a complete cleansing. With increased knowledge and experience, baptism by immersion taught additional truths regarding his relationship to the Savior. These truths included: I want to follow the Savior; He died and lived again, as I also can; a rebirth is required for true discipleship, and without the baptism of fire (the gift of the Holy Ghost), immersion in water alone signifies nothing. These are only some of the possible deeper meanings that could have touched the understanding of this man as he considered the rich symbol of baptism by immersion.

Greater Truths through Righteous Living

Every symbol of the temple, in a like manner, can bring us greater understanding of the Savior, our relationship to him, and our place in the plan of salvation. This process depends on the individual's spiritual growth and experience in life, occurring in parallel with their regular temple activity. If, for example, the young man above were baptized at age eight, and never returned to church again, never received the priesthood, never served a mission, or developed a testimony, his response at age forty to the question of why he was baptized by immersion would no doubt be the same as it was at age eight. He might say, "Well, I was baptized by immersion, those many years ago, to wash away all my sins".

There would have been no increase in his understanding of the rich symbol of baptism by immersion. He would be exactly where he was as an eight-year-old.

The same would be true for any member of the Church who goes only once to the temple and rarely, if ever, returns. In some cases, people would love to go to the temple more often but cannot because of health or other reasons. However, for any member who chooses not to go, his understanding of the symbols of the temple and the great truths that these symbols can teach would be limited to his first and only impression gained on the day when he received his endowment.

The first visit to the temple can be a little overwhelming and even confusing. A wonderful spirit is felt, but everything is so new and so different that it is impossible to ponder all the rich symbolism that is presented. These first visits are usually a preamble to leaving on a mission or preparing for a temple sealing. The excitement that surrounds these events often detracts from one's ability to focus on the deeper messages of the endowment. It is for this reason that we are counseled to return often to the temple. Regular temple attendance not only increases the vicarious work for the dead, but it allows repeated exposure to the richest symbolic teachings that are available for man, teachings that contain all the knowledge of godliness.

Just as the many levels of understanding associated with baptism by immersion are learned as one personally progresses in gospel activity, the same is true of all the symbols of the temple. They will only teach greater truths if we are striving to live our lives according to the gospel outside the temple and then attend the temple in order to ponder and learn from the symbols over time. The process is not unlike the Savior using parables during his ministry to teach his disciples deeper truths of the kingdom.

> And the disciples came, and said unto him, Why speakest thou unto them in parables?
>
> He answered and said unto them, Because it is given unto you to know the mysteries of the kingdom of heaven, but to them it is not given.
>
> For whosoever hath, to him shall be given, and he shall have more abundance: but whosoever hath not, from him shall be taken away even that he hath.
>
> Therefore speak I to them in parables: because they seeing see not; and hearing they hear not, neither do they understand. . . .
>
> But blessed are your eyes, for they see: and your ears, for they hear. (Matthew 13:10–16)

The Savior's use of parables was not to make his teaching easier to understand. Christ taught in parables so that those who were spiritually prepared could be taught the deeper mysteries of the kingdom. Those who had eyes could see, and those who had ears could hear. Those who were spiritually unprepared would see and hear only the most superficial meaning of the parable and gain nothing from the experience. In a like manner, temple symbols will reveal the "mysteries of Godliness" only to the degree we have prepared ourselves for this greater understanding. It is a lifelong process and will never end as long as we return to the temple seeking greater light as we participate in this most sacred work.

NOTES

1. Harold B. Lee, *Ye Are the Light of the World* (Salt Lake City: Deseret Book, 1974), chapter 25.

2. Boyd K. Packer, *The Holy Temple* (Salt Lake City: Bookcraft, 1980), 39.

3. Joseph Smith, *The History of The Church of Jesus Christ of Latter-day Saints*, ed. B.H. Roberts, vol. 5 (Salt Lake City: Deseret Book, 1950), 499.

Chapter Five

ALL STAND AS ONE

S ister Early was one of our most faithful temple patrons. We would
see her every week at the same time and on the same session. It was
always a joy to greet her and thank her for her service. This particular
afternoon she stopped as she was about to leave.

"President, I was just told by Sister Frank that we are asked not to
kneel in the temple when we have a personal prayer. I can't kneel anyway
because of my arthritis, but I'm not sure I understand this. Isn't the temple
a 'house of prayer'? What better place could there be to kneel and open our
hearts to the Lord?"

Her question was sincere, and I wanted to answer it in the best possible way.

"Sister Early, the temple is a house of prayer, and I stand as a witness
of this in my own life. I think the request that we not kneel has to do with
others that may be in the temple. I believe a quiet prayer, offered without
any outward display, is more appropriate for the temple. I think if you
consider this a little, you will come to the same conclusion."

I thanked her again for her faithful service and as she left, I could see
she was giving much thought to what I had said.

QUESTION TO PONDER:

Would kneeling really be so bad as we offered personal prayer in the temple? Or is there a greater principle being taught as we consider this policy of procedure?

In the dedicatory prayer of the Kirtland Temple, we learn many of the functions of the temple: "Organize yourselves; prepare every needful thing, and establish a house, even a house of prayer, a house of fasting, a house of faith, a house of learning, a house of glory, a house of order, a house of God" (D&C 109:9).

It is not by chance that "house of prayer" is listed as the first of these special temple functions. Many go to the temple to pray and ponder conditions present in everyday life. Many leaders go to the temple in a spirit of prayer to seek direction in managing their stewardship. Countless young men and women have sought confirmation in the temple as they prayerfully considered whom to choose as their eternal companion. The quiet reverence of the temple and the moments presented for personal reflection and meditation are an invitation to pray. Prayer always has been and always will be a central part of the temple experience.

Pray in Secret

Personal prayer and kneeling naturally go together. There is no more humbling position than for a person to kneel on the ground and supplicate the Lord. The temple is His holy house. It might seem completely appropriate that in this holy place, one should feel comfortable in kneeling to pray. It was this precise line of reasoning that prompted the question from Sister Early. Why not kneel in the temple to pray? There are at least two reasons why we should not kneel to pray in the temple.

The Savior gave very specific instruction regarding personal prayer. As recorded in Matthew:

> And when thou prayest, thou shalt not be as the hypocrites are: for they love to pray standing in the synagogues and in the corners of the streets, that they may be seen of men. Verily I say unto you, They have their reward.
>
> But thou, when thou prayest, enter into thy closet, and when thou hast shut thy door, pray to thy Father which is in secret; and thy Father which seeth in secret shall reward thee openly. (Matthew 6:5-6)

Regardless of how earnest or heartfelt a prayer may be, it would be impossible to kneel in one of the rooms of the temple and not be "seen of men." The Lord teaches that personal prayer should be "in secret" and behind a closed door. There are no private rooms in the temple. There is no practical way that men or women could locate themselves in the temple, offer a kneeling prayer to the Lord, and not be viewed by others.

In addition, a kneeling prayer offered in one of the holy rooms of the temple would bring much attention to the individual. In a sense, it would be as if he were exhibiting his personal worship of God, putting on a display of his faith as he offers up prayer and thanksgiving. He would become the object of attention in the temple. Other patrons in the temple would have their attention drawn to these outward displays of worship. The sacred ordinances and symbolic teaching would become secondary to the actions of a few.

In the book of Alma, an account of the Zoramite's method of worship is recorded. They had corrupted prayer in their synagogues by having all attention directed to a single person offering a scripted and self-righteous monologue that had become their central method of worship. In Alma we read:

> For they had a place built up in the center of their synagogue, a place for standing, which was high above the head; and the top thereof would only admit one person.
>
> Therefore, whosoever desired to worship must go forth and stand upon the top thereof, and stretch forth his hands towards heaven, and cry with a loud voice, saying:
>
> Holy, holy God; we believe that thou art God, and we believe that thou art holy. (Alma 31:13–15).

This is an extreme example of the complete corruption of prayer in a house of worship. When Alma saw this, his heart was grieved. Now imagine a man today, kneeling in the temple in plain view of others, and offering up a prayer to the Lord. In a less extreme, but somewhat similar way, he would be drawing all attention to his public display of worship. This is not the order in the kingdom of God.

Prayer in the temple must be private and not draw any attention to the individual or group of individuals through any outward display. It is done while sitting quietly in the temple. Public prayer is only appropriate when it is offered on behalf of those who are gathered for a worship service or other meeting. The instruction, therefore, that one not kneel in the temple to offer personal prayers is consistent with the Savior's invitation to "pray to thy Father which is in secret."

All Are Equal Before the Lord

There is, however, a higher principle of temple insight taught through this policy of procedure. To understand this higher order of procedure, one must first realize that in the temple all are equal. Equality before God is a fundamental principle of the gospel of mercy. Among God's children there is great inequality of capacity, of opportunity, of intellect, of physical gifts, and of resources. But fundamental to the doctrine of the plan of happiness is that each son and daughter of God is equal before the Lord and will have an equal opportunity to make choices that can bring eternal life. This principle of equality is taught by Elder John A. Widtsoe,

> The equality of opportunity which characterizes the plan of salvation is shown in the fact that all the ordinances of the Church, from the highest to the lowest, are available to every person who enters the Church. Faith, repentance, baptism, and the gift of the Holy Ghost, are, for all, the four cardinal principles and ordinances for active participation in the work of the Church, irrespective of the powers of men. The endowments of the temple, and all the blessings that may there be received, are available to every member of the Church who has shown himself active in the faith. In fundamental principles, in

gifts and blessings, in spiritual opportunities, as required or offered by the Church, men are stripped of all differences, and stand as if they were equal before God. This is equality of opportunity.[1]

In the temple we are "stripped of all differences" and stand "equal before God." This is the founding principle of the law of mercy. A loving Father in Heaven has provided a way for all his children to stand as equals as far as their opportunity to receive all the blessings of exaltation. Just as we all stand as equal in terms of opportunity before God, we stand as equals in the temple. Nothing that any individual does in the temple should bring special attention to him. Elder Boyd K. Packer emphasizes this same equality in the temple as he discusses temple dress, "When we do ordinance work in the temple we wear white clothing. This clothing is symbolic of purity and worthiness and cleanliness. As you put your clothing in the locker you leave your cares and concerns and distractions there with them. You step out of this private little dressing area dressed in white and you feel a oneness and a sense of equality, for all around you are similarly dressed."[2]

The order of the temple is that we feel a sense of "oneness and a sense of equality." Any behavior or action that would make one stand out in the temple, that would draw people's attention away from the temple ordinance, is contrary to the spirit of the temple. For example, a very loud voice, causing all eyes to turn to the source, would be inconsistent with the reverence of the temple. Extreme make-up, lavish jewelry, or even strongly scented perfume could cause unwanted attention that would distract others from the holy symbols and sacred ordinances being performed in the temple. Even extreme or flamboyant gestures by an ordinance worker could serve as a distraction for patrons who have come to the temple to feel the oneness and equality that should always be present. Elder Orson F. Whitney teaches this principle of equality as it relates to the opportunities for all of God's children, "The poor man is the equal of the rich man when he stands before God and asks, What must I do to be saved? There is no purchasing our way into the kingdom of heaven; money can buy many things, but it cannot buy membership in the

Church of Christ; it cannot buy the principles of truth, the blessings of the Gospel, the gifts of the Holy Ghost. All men are equal before God in respect of these things."[3]

There is no place in the kingdom of God that offers a greater sense of equality than in the temple. Men are not equal in abilities or opportunities, but all are equal before God. Each is equal in his opportunity to experience the ordinances that can qualify them to return to the presence of the Lord. In the temple, the learned sit next to the illiterate, and the rich sit next to the poor; those with lofty callings and great experience sit next to the newest and least experienced of the kingdom. All are dressed in white. All are the same before God. Each is participating in a holy work and doing for others what they cannot do for themselves. Each will learn at his own pace and according to his spiritual understanding and preparation. Every behavior or action, our dress, our language, the volume and tone of our voice, and even our personal prayers, should promote this feeling of equality and oneness that is part of being in the temple. Eyes should not be on any individual in the temple. All eyes and hearts should be on the sacred ordinances that are performed by the living for the dead and on the rich symbolic narrative that is part of temple worship.

NOTES

1. John A. Widtsoe, *Rational Theology* (Salt Lake City: Deseret Book, 1937), 140.

2. Packer, *The Holy Temple*, 71.

3. Orson F. Witney, General Conference Report, April 5, 1909, 74.

Chapter Six

THE VEIL PARTS

I t was one of the first times I would use my sealing powers, and I was a little nervous. Sister Gunn had asked me to do some of her family names. I was honored. The session went quickly, and the Spirit was very strong. It was obvious to all of us that these names meant a great deal to Sister Gunn. As we left the sealing room I could tell that she was waiting until everyone had left to talk to me. Since the sealer is always the last one to leave, she had to wait a few minutes as the others cleared the room. As I approached her, she offered this question in a very low voice, "Did you see her?"

"See whom?" I replied.

"My Aunt Joy. She was there." She pointed to one of the chairs on the west wall of the sealing room. "As we did her work I saw her during the entire ordinance, and then she was gone. It was wonderful. I will never forget the joy on her face."

She stared, waiting for my response. This was not the first time I had received a report of the veil parting for a brief moment in the temple. I knew Sister Gunn very well. I had been her bishop years earlier. She was a strong and spiritually mature member of the Church, who had raised a great family. I had no doubt that what she reported was exactly what had happened.

"I did not see her, but I think it was intended that only you should see her. Thank you for sharing this with me."

She waved slightly as she proceeded to the locker area. Her countenance radiated pure joy.

QUESTION TO PONDER:

These marvelous spiritual manifestations are occurring in temples all over the world. Why not collect, document and report them? Couldn't such an audit inspire and bless others to come to the temple?

No church on the earth today believes more fervently in spiritual manifestations than The Church of Jesus Christ of Latter-day Saints. The seventh article of faith declares our belief in prophecy, revelation, and visions: "We believe in the gift of tongues, prophecy, revelation, visions, healing, interpretation of tongues, and so forth."

The Restoration of the Church began with the visit of God the Father and his Son, Jesus Christ, to the boy prophet, Joseph Smith, in 1820. The coming forth of the Book of Mormon, the restoration of the Priesthood, and the restoring of all the priesthood keys required the visit of heavenly messengers. A fundamental right that each member of the Church enjoys is the promise of personal revelation; through the power of the Holy Spirit, we can know that the Church is true and that a living prophet presides over this great work.

Help from beyond the Veil

The doctrine of the Church teaches that man existed long before his physical birth into mortality and teaches that death is simply a passing from this probationary life to immortality. The temple offers a sacred connection between mortal life and that which is beyond the veil. Ordinances essential for exaltation must be performed by the living for those have left mortality without such, that they "might be judged according to men in the flesh, but live according to God in the spirit" (1 Peter 4:6).

There have been countless reports of spiritual manifestations where the veil is parted and a connection is made between the mortal and immortal worlds. Many of these reports have been published in personal journals. Some have been published in books or conference reports. For the most part, however, these special spiritual manifestations remain underreported. Elder Widtsoe gives this counsel:

> Divine manifestations for individual comfort may be received by every worthy member of the Church. In that respect all faithful members of the Church are equal. Such manifestations most commonly guide the recipients to the solution of personal problems; though, frequently, they also open the mind to a clearer comprehension of the Lord's vast plan of salvation. They are cherished possessions, and should be so valued by those who receive them. In their very nature, they are sacred and should be so treated.
>
> It is unwise, therefore, for those who have received such manifestations to send copies to others, to relate them by word of mouth in diverse places, and otherwise to scatter abroad a personal, sacred experience.[1]

Elder Boyd K. Packer offers similar counsel, but does allow for the sharing of spiritual manifestations that have occurred in the lives of others from many years earlier: "I have come to know that deeply spiritual experiences are usually given to us for our individual edification and it is best not to talk of them generally. . . . We may be prompted on occasion to tell of our spiritual experiences, but generally we should regard them as sacred. It is not out of order, however, to present some experiences from those who have lived in years past."[2]

The counsel offered by these two apostles is the same; they both teach that these special manifestations are not to be talked of "generally" or related to others by "word of mouth in diverse places." Understanding the reason for this precaution, that spiritual experiences remain private and personal, will add insight into this sacred aspect of temple worship.

Extra-mortal assistance in temple activity has been present since the earliest years of the Restoration. Mention of divine assistance and spiritual intervention in the work of the temples can be found in the dedicatory prayer of the Kirtland Temple as recorded in the

Doctrine and Covenants: "And we ask thee, Holy Father, that thy servants may go forth from this house armed with thy power, and that thy name may be upon them, and thy glory be round about them, and thine angels have charge over them" (D&C 109: 22).

The power, name, and glory of God are upon this sacred work. Angels have charge over the servants that are involved in temple work. Miracles are occurring every day in both the work of identifying those who have passed on, and in the performance of the sacred and exalting ordinances of the temple. Mormon offers additional understanding of how angels minister unto men and what their office of ministry includes. He explains that angels are subject to Christ and minister according to His command. He also explains that angels show themselves to those who are strong in faith and firm in mind and that part of an angel's ministry is to do the work of the covenants of the Father.

> And because he hath done this, my beloved brethren, have miracles ceased? Behold I say unto you, Nay; neither have angels ceased to minister unto the children of men.
> For behold, they are subject unto him, to minister according to the word of his command, showing themselves unto them of strong faith and a firm mind in every form of godliness.
> And the office of their ministry is to call men unto repentance, and to fulfill and to do the work of the covenants of the Father. (Moroni 7: 29–31)

This doctrine taught by Mormon tells much concerning the interaction between the seen and the unseen worlds. The work of angels and their interaction with mortal men as presented by Mormon have everything to do with the temple.

What group within the Church would most closely fit the description of "strong in faith and firm in mind"? It is those who have lived according to sacred covenants and are worthy and qualified to come to the temple to serve. No other subgroup within the Church better fits this description. The strong in faith are those who have been endowed with power through the sacred ordinances of the temple.

What is the "work of the covenants of the Father"? These are all the covenants and promised blessings of Abraham, Isaac, and Jacob—all the sacred covenants that are part of the new and everlasting covenant of the restored gospel. These are the covenants of the temple and the sacred ordinances essential for the exaltation of man. These ordinances and covenants allow man, as Brigham Young said, "to walk back to the presence of the Father, passing the angels who stand as sentinels, being enabled to give them the key words, the signs and tokens, pertaining to the Holy Priesthood, and gain your eternal exaltation."[3]

Faith before Miracles

Not surprisingly, spiritual manifestations occur throughout this great work of the temple. Angels have been assigned from the beginning of temple building in this dispensation to have charge over men and to minister and show themselves to man according to Christ's command.

A part of the question offered at the beginning of this chapter still remains unanswered: why not catalogue and report each and every spiritual manifestation as they occur? To answer this part, we must first consider how these spiritual manifestations occur. Mormon offers the following insight as he explains how miracles happen: "for it is by faith that miracles are wrought; and it is by faith that angels appear and minister unto men; wherefore, if these things have ceased wo be unto the children of men, for it is because of unbelief, and all is vain" (Moroni 7:37).

Miracles are wrought by faith. The question of why these wonderful spiritual manifestations are to be kept sacred and not generally publicized to the world is because they are personal. The miracle that parts the veil and allows a direct connection between those in mortality with those beyond the grave, results from the great faith of the person experiencing the vision. In the case presented at the beginning of this chapter, Sister Gunn was blessed with the opportunity to see her deceased aunt while the sacred sealing ordinance for this aunt was performed. This miracle was possible because of the faith and good works of Sister Gunn. It was intended for her and perhaps for some of her closest family or friends, but it was not intended for a more general audience. It was her faith that allowed it to happen.

Reported in some indiscriminate and public way, this personal occurrence would be of doubtful value and could be misunderstood or undervalued. In one of His strongest expressions of caution regarding sacred things, the Lord said, "Give not that which is holy unto the dogs, neither cast ye your pearls before swine, lest they trample them under their feet, and turn again and rend you" (Matthew 7:6).

One of the most holy experiences in this life is when the veil parts and a connection is made between that which is mortal and that which is immortal. Using the Lord's own language, a spiritual manifestation is a "pearl" of infinite worth and should not be "cast" before the unbeliever. The Savior further suggests that those who are unprepared to receive such knowledge would "trample" these sacred occurrences "under their feet" and "turn again and rend" or belittle the sharing. The sacred appearance that occurred in the life of Sister Gunn on that afternoon was for her benefit only. She may choose to share it with a select few: a family member, a priesthood leader, or a close friend. In each case those who are privileged to hear about it will already share her faith in the important work of the temple and an appreciation of the sacred significance of this wonderful manifestation. Sister Gunn qualified to have an experience like this because of her faith and the work she was doing on behalf of her kindred dead. She was blessed with an increased understanding of the joy her work was causing on the other side of the veil. The blessing was intended principally to strengthen and bless her life and was never intended for a broader audience.

It still might be argued that such a marvelous sign as experienced by Sister Gunn could serve to inspire and motivate others to come to the temple. Furthermore, it might be suggested that a more public sharing of this sacred experience could help the unbeliever. Sister Gunn experienced a miracle, a great sign that confirmed to her the reality of life after death and proved to her, beyond any doubt, that temple work is essential for the progress and happiness of her deceased ancestors. But would publishing or announcing this sign make others more faithful? Does faith come by signs? The Lord offered some very clear counsel on the relationship between signs and faith as he rebuked some of the early Saints in this dispensation:

> And he that seeketh signs shall see signs, but not unto salvation.
>
> Verily, I say unto you, there are those among you who seek signs, and there have been such even from the beginning;
>
> But, behold, faith cometh not by signs, but signs follow those that believe.
>
> Yea, signs come by faith, not by the will of men, nor as they please, but by the will of God.
>
> Yea, signs come by faith, unto mighty works, for without faith no man pleaseth God; and with whom God is angry he is not well pleased; wherefore, unto such he showeth no signs, only in wrath unto their condemnation.
>
> Wherefore, I, the Lord, am not pleased with those among you who have sought after signs and wonders for faith, and not for the good of men unto my glory. (D&C 63:7–12)

It is clear that faith does not come by signs, but that signs "follow those that believe." Sister Gunn believed and demonstrated this belief by her good works, and then there followed a sign. No question her faith was strengthened by what she experienced. The faith of a select few might also be strengthened as she shared what she saw and felt. Reporting or even experiencing a great sign from heaven, however, offers no guarantee that those who experience such will be blessed with greater faith. There are countless examples of this in the scriptures. Consider Nephi's frustration with his older brothers:

> Ye are swift to do iniquity but slow to remember the Lord your God. Ye have seen an angel, and he spake unto you; yea, ye have heard his voice from time to time; and he hath spoken unto you in a still small voice, but ye were past feeling, that ye could not feel his

words; . . . yea, and ye know that by his word he can cause the rough places to be made smooth, and smooth places shall be broken up. O, then, why is it, that ye can be so hard in your hearts? (1 Nephi 17:45–46)

Could anyone have received greater signs than Nephi's older brothers, Laman and Lemuel? They saw an angel and heard his voice; they had seen the power of God, yet their hearts were so hard that they were "past feeling." A sign does not bring a lasting increase in faith nor does it prompt mighty works in one whose heart is unbelieving.

On this point the Lord is very clear; signs come by "faith, unto mighty works." One should not seek, or in the case of spiritual man-ifestations, publish signs and wonders to promote faith in others. This has never been and will never be the order of heaven. In this rebuke the Lord declares that He is not pleased with those who want a sign to have faith. The sign Sister Gunn experienced surely augmented her faith, but it did not cause her to be faithful; her faith was already strong. This is the divine order. First, a demonstration of faith and good works, and then, according to the will of God, a sign may follow.

This same doctrine is taught by Moroni in the book of Ether.

And now, I, Moroni, would speak somewhat concerning these things; I would show unto the world that faith is things which are hoped for and not seen; wherefore, dispute not because ye see not, for ye receive no witness until after the trial of your faith.(Ether 12:6)

Again the pattern was mentioned: first, a trial of faith, and then the things of God may be seen. The Lord himself declared to the brother of Jared that it was by his faith that he was allowed to look upon the pre-mortal Christ as recorded in the book of Ether:

And the Lord said unto him: Because of thy faith thou hast seen that I shall take upon me flesh and blood; and never has man come before me with such exceeding faith as thou hast. (Ether 3:9)

The miracle of seeing the Lord was brought about by the "exceed-ing faith" of the brother of Jared. Any attempt to publish or make public in any way the sacred and personal spiritual manifestations of the temple to give faith to others would be contrary to this divine order. The many spiritual manifestations that are occurring in temples all over the world are, therefore, to be kept sacred and private. They are the result of an individual's great faith and good works and are given to that individual for his personal blessing. These manifestations, shared in a more public way, may lead skeptics to belittle or trivialize that which is holy.

Paul teaches this great principle of sacred and holy things being limited to those who are spiritually prepared to receive them and learn from them. He teaches that sharing too freely may be viewed by the spiritually unprepared as "foolishness." These sacred manifestations must be received "by the spirit which is of God," and cannot be understood by the "spirit of the world."

> Now we have received, not the spirit of the world, but the spirit which is of God; that we might know the things that are freely given to us of God.
>
> Which things also we speak, not in the words which man's wisdom teacheth, but which the Holy Ghost teacheth; comparing spiritual things with spiritual.
>
> But the natural man receiveth not the things of the Spirit of God: for they are foolishness unto him: neither can he know them, because they are spiritually discerned. (1 Corinthians 2:12–14)

These sacred experiences and all that is holy in the temple require spiritual preparation. As Paul teaches, they must be "spiritually discerned." Spiritual discernment requires a believing heart and a certain level of spiritual maturity. It is for this reason that a significant period of time is needed before a new member goes to the temple to receive the endowment. Without adequate time for spiritual preparation, there could be no spiritual discernment of the sacredness of the temple covenants. This is why we do not speak of sacred things outside the temple. It has nothing to do with keeping secrets from the world. Without spiritual discernment, the sacred and holy ordinances and spiritual manifestations of the temple would be belittled, mocked, or dismissed by the wisdom of an unbelieving world. Sharing sacred experiences with those who are not prepared or qualified to receive such knowledge will not build faith in the unbeliever.

Spiritual manifestations will continue to be a regular part of the temple experience for the faithful. There is a divine promise that angels will minister and show themselves to men in the great work of redeeming the dead. This holy intervention from beyond the veil will be kept sacred and will continue to bless lives according to the faithfulness and good works of those engaged in temple service.

NOTES

1. John A. Widtsoe, *Evidences and Reconciliations* (Salt Lake City: Bookcraft, 1960), 98–99.

2. Packer, *The Holy Temple*, 243.

3. Brigham Young, *Journal of Discourses*, 2:31, Apr. 6, 1858.

Chapter Seven

A PERFECT SESSION

B*rother Lemon had just officiated the 6:00 P.M. session and looked happy as he came down the hall heading for the office. It was obvious he was having a good day.*

"Good session, Brother Lemon?" I asked, seeing the big smile on his face.

He responded enthusiastically, "A perfect session, President, every seat was full, and everyone knew what they were doing. We are truly becoming a temple-going people. I don't think any of us had to help anyone during the whole session. It went as smooth as possible. It couldn't have been easier."

I was happy for Brother Lemon, but as he entered the office to have the ordinance cards scanned, his words, "It couldn't have been easier" and his assessment that the session had been "perfect" bothered me just a little.

QUESTION TO PONDER:

Why is a session where no one needs help and everything proceeds easily not "perfect"?

Brother Lemon was very pleased with the session he had just officiated. Everyone on the session was experienced in temple work. No help was needed, and everything went smoothly. In his mind it was a "perfect session," offering clear evidence that many of the Saints in the temple district were becoming a temple-going people. However, from our perspective as a temple presidency, a perfect session would have looked a little different.

A Perfect Session

A perfect session from our point of view would also have every seat filled, as in Brother Lemon's session, but half of those sitting in the session would be unsure of themselves and in need of some assistance. They would be in the temple after a long absence or perhaps attending for only their second or third time. The other half of this hypothetically perfect session would be made up of a friend sitting beside each inexperienced patron. This friend would be knowledgeable of temple procedure and would provide support and companionship for his less experienced partner. This would indeed be a perfect session.

Temple sessions where there are many needing assistance, accompanied by friends to encourage and support their attendance, is the single strongest indicator that a temple district is growing and vibrant. It means that wards and stakes in this district will grow stronger as more people come to the temple. Bishops and stake presidents will see and feel the difference in their organizations as temple attendance increases. President Howard W. Hunter offers this insight: "Increased temple attendance will result in stronger families. Many of our temples are still underused, except on weekends. Much work remains to be done, and we continue to encourage you to attend the temple as often as is feasible. Stronger marriages, more attentive parents, and more faithful children will come as a result of following this counsel."[1]

There will be greater love, sacrifice, and service within the kingdom as more of our members come to the temple. A perfect session, therefore, would always include many who are just beginning the journey of learning to worship in the temple.

Filling the Temple

What might be done to increase the likelihood of having a temple filled with sessions that are perfect, as described above? To answer this question, we must first examine current temple activity. The Reno Nevada Temple district includes eight stakes and about 6,000 current temple recommend holders. If every seat in every session was filled all year long, the temple could complete about 54,000 endowments. At present this temple is doing a little less than half that number, about 24,000. These 24,000 endowments are done by three groups of people: the general membership of the stakes, the ordinance workers, and the weekly temple patrons. The following table gives the approximate contribution of each of these groups over a one-year period:

Group	Number of Persons	Endowments Done
General Membership	5,600	16,000
Ordinance Workers	320	6,000
Weekly Temple Patrons	80	2,000
Total	6,000	24,000

The general membership of the eight stakes of my temple district is averaging about three endowment visits to the temple a year per individual. Clearly, some of these 5,600 individuals come much more often than three times a year and others do not come at all. The general membership completes about 16,000 endowments a year.

The ordinance workers who carry out the work of the temple have been called and set apart by the temple presidency. They are a highly trained group and are able to administer the sacred ordinances of the temple correctly and with great love. The average age for ordinance workers in this small temple is over seventy years. They come from all occupations including teachers, businessmen, doctors, lawyers, ranchers, dairymen, and many, many great-grandmothers and great-grandfathers. It takes about 320 ordinance workers to carry out the work of this temple. It is very common for ordinance workers to be sent on a session during their shift in the temple, as both a blessing for them and to fill in when attendance at a particular session is low. This group contributes about 6,000 endowments a year.

The final group is made up of those who faithfully come every week to do temple work, many for their own ancestors. They are in the temple each week on the same day and in the same sessions. They are well-known to the ordinance workers, to the office staff, and to the members of the presidency. They have caught the full vision of family history work, and they come month after month and year after year with their hearts fully turned to their fathers as they accomplish hundreds of ordinances for their kindred dead. They are an inspiring group that understand and love the temple at a depth that is born out of faithful and long service in the Lord's house. These weekly temple patrons contribute about 2,000 endowments a year.

Filling the Temple

As mentioned above, with about 6,000 temple recommend holders, our small temple operates at about a 50 percent capacity. This is an outstanding percentage, but what needs to be done to fill the other 50 percent of the seats and, thereby, create many perfect sessions? What would be required to increase our temple attendance to 100 percent capacity? To answer this question, first consider three common reasons why members with temple recommends do not come to the temple more often:

1. I don't have enough time. There are just too many other things competing for those 2 to 2½ that are required to do a session in the temple.
2. I have no way to get there. I don't own a car, and there is no bus service available to the temple. Besides, I don't like going alone.
3. The temple confuses me a little bit. I'm not sure what I'm doing and I always need lots of help with everything. It's embarrassing.

There are other very good and very legitimate reasons for not going to the temple, issues like health, childcare, and an incompatible work schedule. But these three particular reasons listed above disappear when experienced temple patrons invite friends to come to the temple.

1. "I don't have enough time"

The first reason is eliminated because going to the temple would become a social outing for one couple invited by another, or for one member of a quorum or group invited by another. If a couple traditionally have a date night once a month to go to the temple, it would be very easy to include another couple. The couple invited would not look at the temple activity as taking time away, but would view it as a night of sharing with another couple. It would not only be a temple visit, but it would take the priority of special time spent together with friends. When a member of an elders quorum receives a special invitation to attend the temple with one of his friends, the visit takes on an interpersonal importance where a friendship is nurtured and men do something worthy and important together. Under these favorable conditions, it would be easy to combine a visit to the temple with an additional activity such as dinner or a quick breakfast together.

2. "I have no way to get there."

The second objection is also eliminated by offering to bring someone to the temple. A significant number of individuals in every ward just don't have the means for getting themselves to the temple. They are thrilled when someone remembers them and includes them in a temple outing. Once those who regularly go to the temple adopt the practice of always prayerfully inviting someone to go with them, they will be guided by the spirit to reach out to this group who cannot otherwise find a way to the temple. Lives will be blessed on both sides of this equation. Those receiving the invitation will be blessed by regularly being invited to the temple. They will not only participate in the sacred ordinances and enjoy the many blessings of temple service, but they will also feel included, loved, and supported by others. Those who do the inviting will be blessed immediately by the gratitude they will receive for this small but significant act of kindness.

3. "I always need lots of help. It's embarrassing."

The third reason for not going to the temple is perhaps the most tragic. These individuals are uncomfortable with the temple ordinances since they are unsure of what to do and how to do it. The longer they stay away from returning to temple activity, the more daunting the temple becomes in their hearts and minds. It becomes something mysterious and strange. This is lifted from them instantly when an understanding friend simply says, "Come with me to the temple. I would love to sit with you and help you." One or two visits to the temple with a friend are all that is needed for someone to feel the peace and the joy of serving in the House of the Lord and forget the uneasiness he once felt. This is such a small sacrifice for the active temple patron to make and will mean so much in the life of the member who has a friend by his side. As mentioned above, these invitations should be guided by prayer. No act of kindness has greater spiritual significance than helping someone begin a life that includes regular temple worship. Lives will be blessed forever, both for those doing the inviting and those being invited.

If the approximately 6,000 temple recommend holders in the Reno Nevada temple district made the decision to always bring someone with them when they came to the temple, this small temple would reach and exceed 100 percent capacity in one short year. "Come with me" or "Come with us" to the temple is such a wonderful invitation, an invitation where no obligation or command is implied or felt. It is consistent with the free-will offering that temple service should always reflect. It is an invitation to share sacred experiences found in the Church. The result of friends coming to the temple together in greater numbers will increase the amount of temple attendance. This increase will be the result of an invitation being offered under the guidance of the Holy Spirit.

Other ways to increase temple attendance are also possible.

Successful stake and ward temple days result in large numbers of temple ordinances being performed. Members make great sacrifices to support their leaders and be in the temple on these occasions. Many come for the first time in years because of these efforts. Temple recommends are renewed after years of neglect. Family history cards that have been forgotten are dusted off and brought to the temple as a stake mobilizes all its worthy members to come. When these special temple dates are set by a ward or stake, many members, for the first time, prepare to receive their temple ordinances. This alone makes these occasions particularly special for those in attendance.

These special events should continue under the direction and inspiration of local priesthood leaders and in cooperation with the temple presidency. Imagine the increase in temple activity that could be realized in one small temple district if the efforts of local priesthood leaders were combined with the commitment of those attending the temple to always bring a friend. The number of sessions would have to be increased, and eventually, more temples would have to be built.

Opposition

It would be an oversight to discuss effective ways to increase temple activity and not offer this word of warning: with every effort to build temples or to increase temple attendance, forces of evil will inevitably arise to destroy these efforts. The possibility of my small temple operating at or near full capacity can become a reality, but there will be storms of opposition. Since the earliest days of the Restoration, Satan and his minions have opposed the work of the temple. Consider the colorful words of Brigham Young, "Some say, 'I do not like to do it, for we never began to build a Temple without the bells of hell beginning to ring.' I want to hear them ring again. All the tribes of hell will be on the move, if we uncover the walls of this Temple."[2]

The "bells of hell" will ring to rally evil against any effort to establish a holy temple on the earth or to carry out the sacred ordinances performed therein. The reason for this is that the very presence of a temple reduces the power of evil. A temple can call down from heaven the power of God to reduce the influence of Satan as taught by Elder George Q Cannon: "Every foundation stone that is laid for a temple, and every temple completed according to the order the Lord has revealed for His holy priesthood, lessens the power of Satan on the earth, and increases the power of God and godliness, moves the heavens in mighty power in our behalf, invokes and calls down upon us the blessings of eternal gods, and those who reside in their presence."[3]

This opposition is real and can be felt from the moment a temple is announced. These forces of darkness, however, are not limited to just the period of construction or the opening of a new temple; very real opposition to temple activity continues as long as the temple is in operation, whether it is directed against the efforts of a stake to plan a special temple day or against one person's decision to invite another to go to the temple. One of Satan's most effective tools is to incite a person against that which is good. Consider the following experience as recorded by a member of a local stake presidency during the announcement and building of our small temple:

> Our stake presidency had received permission to identify a piece of land in our community for the construction of a temple. Words cannot describe the joy and excitement we felt as we began this very confidential search. Quickly a perfect parcel of land was identified and a price was informally agreed upon. Officials from the temple department, as well as members of the Seventy, came and approved the purchase. Our assignment was to prepare a pamphlet that was to be distributed to land developers and homeowners in the area so that appropriate zoning modification could go forward without objection.
>
> Almost immediately there was a groundswell of opposition. Many objections were presented including legitimate concerns about parking, possible noise, and an increase in traffic. Some of the concerns were irrational such as fear that the superb landscaping of the temple would reflect negatively on the properties in the surrounding area and fear of offensive smells or strange noises associated with the "secret works" being performed in the temple. Members from the local stake went door to door to every home within a reasonable

distance of the site to offer personal assurances regarding the temple. Hundreds of pamphlets were distributed, but the opposition grew in intensity. Some of those who lived closest to the site were quoted as saying that they would lie their bodies down in front of the earth moving equipment if any attempt was made to begin construction.

Finally, word came from the temple department and the Seventy that we were to abandon this site and find a new one. A beautiful piece of property was immediately identified. It was high on a hill with easy access from the interstate highway. The size of the property was larger than the original site and cost about a third as much. Approval was quickly granted, and the temple was finished about a year and a half later.

Thousands of people came to the open house to see the temple before its dedication. A counselor in the bishopric of the ward where the original site was located reported that one of the neighbors, who had threatened to lie down in front of the tractors rather than allow the construction of the temple to begin, had attended the open house and said the following at a home owners meeting.

"I really don't know what came over me. I'm not sure why I objected to that beautiful building being built in our neighborhood."

This is a perfect example of how the forces of evil can incite people against that which is good. Consider these words of Nephi as he speaks of the power of Satan in the latter days,

> At that day shall he rage in the hearts of the children of men, and stir them up to anger against that which is good.
>
> And others will he pacify, and lull them away into carnal security, . . . and thus the devil cheateth their souls, and leadeth them away carefully down to hell. . . .
>
> And thus he whispereth in their ears, until he grasps them with his awful chains, from whence there is no deliverance. (2 Nephi 28:20–22)

Good people were stirred up "against that which is good" without even understanding by what power this had happened. Later, as this nonmember neighbor honestly reflected on her objections to the building of the temple in her neighborhood, she could not explain nor understand her extreme and opposing behavior. Elder

Boyd K. Packer teaches that this force of opposition to the holy and sacred work of temples is not limited only to those who are outside the faith. He warns that the personal apathy of members may be one of the adversary's most effective tools to "pacify and lull" us into "carnal security."

> Temples are the very center of the spiritual strength of the Church. We should expect that the adversary will try to interfere with us as a Church and with us individually as we seek to participate in this sacred and inspired work. The interference can vary from the terrible persecutions of the earlier days to apathy toward the work. The latter is perhaps the most dangerous and debilitating form of resistance to temple work.[4]

It must be recognized that at almost every level of temple activity there will exist opposition in one form or another. This will be particularly true when a special effort is made to increase temple activity. Father Lehi taught that opposition always has and always will be part of our mortal struggle.

> For it must needs be, that there is an opposition in all things. If not so, my first-born in the wilderness, righteousness could not be brought to pass, neither wickedness, neither holiness nor misery, neither good nor bad . . . , having no life neither death, nor corruption nor incorruption, happiness nor misery, neither sense nor insensibility (2 Nephi 2:11).

Since temples represent the most holy sanctuaries on earth and since the ordinances performed therein are essential to help man return to the presence of God, the forces of evil will manifest to the same intensity in opposition to this sacred work. Once the reality of this opposition is understood by those who are involved in temple work, opposition can be anticipated, it can be recognized, and it can be overcome. It is only when the source of the opposition is not recognized that Satan gains his advantage.

NOTES

1. *The Teachings of Howard W. Hunter*, ed. Clyde J. Williams (Salt Lake City: Deseret Book, 1997), 241.

2. *Journal of Discourses*, vol. 8. 356.

3. George Q. Cannon, Logan Temple Dedication, 1877. Reported in Boyd K. Packer, *The Holy Temple*, 179.

4. Packer, *The Holy Temple*, 177.

Chapter Eight

DIVINE KNOWLEDGE

B lain and I had known each other for years. I had delivered many of
his grandchildren, and our families were very close. I could see that
he was concerned about something as he entered my office.

He began, "Something happened last night that really bothered me,
and I want to talk to you about it."

I encouraged him to go on.

He continued, "I visited Brother Johns last night. He is what we used
to call a senior Aaronic priesthood holder and has been inactive for many
years. The bishop had asked me to give him a visit since his mother died
recently, and the ward had helped with the funeral arrangements. The
bishop thought it might be a good time to invite him back to activity. At
first everything went well. My companion, Brother Shears, was sharing his testimony of the great blessings that come through full activity in
the Church. He then mentioned to Brother Johns that a temple had been
recently built in our small city and that we could now enjoy all the sacred
blessings of the temple without having to drive to Oakland. He mentioned
to Brother Johns that through the sacred ordinances of the temple he could
be sealed to his family, forever.

"At this point Brother Johns shocked us both when he declared that he
knew all about the temple. He then proceeded to describe in some detail
all that we do in the temple. He described our temple clothing and much
of what is contained in the endowment. We were both shocked, to say the
least. I asked him how he had obtained this information. He explained

that it was all on the Internet and that anyone could look it up if they so desired. President, there was a dark spirit in that house as he declared to us: 'There is nothing in your temple that I do not already know'."

Blain continued, "I had trouble sleeping last night, president. I had no idea that all of our temple ordinances have been revealed to the world. Doesn't this in some way defile the temple?"

I could see the sincere anguish in his question and I assured him that the holy work of the temple and the sacred ordinances performed could never be defiled by the actions of apostates. I told him that I was aware that such sites were available, but that I had never cared to visit them and knew that they had nothing to do with my personal worship within the temple. I promised him that Brother Johns could never know through the Internet the sacred truths that were available through regular temple attendance.

QUESTION TO PONDER:

What is the difference between the knowledge we can gain by attending the temple and the knowledge an unbeliever might gain in viewing a website where the sacred ordinances of the temple have been revealed?

I assured Blain that Brother Johns would never come to know the truths of the temple through an Internet site. To understand why I could be so confident in making this statement, we must clearly understand the difference between divine knowledge and secular knowledge.

The knowledge gained in the temple is divine. Divine knowledge is essential to spiritually nourish the soul of man and differs from secular knowledge in several important ways. The following two missionary experiences illustrate the distinction between knowing the things of God through secular learning or through divine learning.

Secular Knowledge

We decided to knock doors in one of the wealthiest areas of the city. After being rejected at many homes, we came to the house of Mr. Ramirez. He answered the door, and I held up a copy of the Book of Mormon and said, "Sir, I have in my hand a history of your people. It explains how they arrived on this continent and where they came from. It teaches of the great civilization they became and how they were eventually destroyed. Most important, it teaches of the visit of Jesus Christ to these people 2,000 years ago. May we come in and share this book with you?"

He immediately invited us in and led us to an office at the rear of his beautiful home. On entering the office, it was obvious he had a great interest in ancient American history. There were archeological relics, maps, and books scattered over a large table in the middle of the room. He then explained to us of his great personal interest in the origins of his people and said he was very interested to hear what we had to teach.

We began to teach Mr. Ramirez about the Book of Mormon. He gladly accepted a copy and invited us to return with the promise we would bring filmstrips and pamphlets that would add understanding about the origin of the book. We visited him weekly and shared everything we had about the Book of Mormon. He read the book with great enthusiasm. After several weeks he offered the following comment prior to the lesson. "I want to thank you young men for bringing this book into my home. I have now read it and believe that it does contain an accurate history of my people. Everything you have taught me and everything I have found on reading the book agrees with my earlier research on the matter. This book will take a place of importance in my library."

We were thrilled to hear what we believed to be a testimony of the Book of Mormon. With his sincere declaration of appreciation, we proceeded to challenge him to baptism. My companion began, "Brother Ramirez, if you believe the book to be true, then you must also believe that Joseph Smith, the young prophet who brought this book to the world through the powers of heaven, must be a prophet of God."

He responded quickly, "I have no doubt that he was a prophet to bring such truth to the world."

My companion continued, "If Joseph was a prophet, then the church he established by the same power would have to be the true church of God."

Brother Ramirez simply nodded his head in apparent agreement. Encouraged by what I was observing, I offered the following, "Brother Ramirez, would you let us teach you more about this wonderful Church, and if you came to know that it was the true Church of God, would you consider being baptized into our faith?"

An uncomfortable quiet settled over the room. Brother Ramirez then spoke, and his tone had changed,

"Young men, I am a Catholic and have been my entire life. My parents and wife and all our family are Catholics. I have no intention of ever leaving my faith. I am grateful for the book you have given me, but I think our time together is over."

He then stood and directed us to the front door of the house and bid us farewell. My companion and I started walking down the street disappointed and confused over what had just happened to our "golden contact."

Consider another missionary experience regarding the divine truth of the Book of Mormon:

Divine Knowledge

We were the first missionaries to teach the gospel to the people of this small village in Mexico. Pablo and his wife and children lived in a small adobe hut with a thatched roof. Pablo was not an educated man and had never learned to read, but his wife helped him by reading from the pamphlets we left and from the Book of Mormon that we had given them. They listened to our message and were the first to be baptized in our small branch.

I was transferred from that small village to the north of the mission and a year passed before I was able to return. On assignment I returned to Pablo's branch on a Sunday. Pablo was now serving in the branch presidency and spoke in the sacrament meeting. He shared his testimony about the Book of Mormon. He held up the book we had given his family a year earlier. The first one hundred pages showed great signs of wear from regular use. The other four hundred pages looked as though they had never been opened. He explained to the small congregation that with the help of his wife, he had finished the first one hundred pages of the Book of Mormon. With great detail and even greater conviction he told us of the events of those first one hundred pages and then testified that the book was the word of God, and that Joseph Smith had to be a prophet to have brought such truth into the world.

After the meeting we went with Pablo to his small adobe house to visit. He was a changed man. Although his job had not changed and his financial situation was exactly as it had been a year earlier, he had expanded his small home with a single room addition that was open and cool. He had partly fenced his yard and now kept a few chickens. He wife explained that as a member of the branch presidency, Pablo wore a clean white shirt each day since he was regularly called on to work with the missionaries. We talked of his experience in learning to read and what the Book of Mormon meant to him. He again declared to those of us who were gathered in his small home on that Sunday afternoon that he knew that the history contained in the book was true and that his Book of Mormon had become one of his most treasured possessions.

Two Ways to Know the Same Truth

These two men both gained knowledge about the Book of Mormon. In terms of substance, we might say their knowledge was the same. Both had read the book. Brother Ramirez was an educated man and had easily read the book from cover to cover in four short weeks. Pablo was initially illiterate and needed the help of his wife to finish the first one hundred pages of the book over the very long period of almost one year. Both believed the Book of Mormon contained a true history of their people and both considered the book to be of great value. The impact of the knowledge they had obtained, however, was very different.

The knowledge Mr. Ramirez had gained of the Book of Mormon caused no change in his life. In fact, he became angry at the notion that his acceptance of the validity of the Book of Mormon should in some way create a desire in him to change. He would certainly be considered a wise man of the world. He had a law degree and was extremely well educated in all aspects of the origin of the ancient inhabitants of Mexico. The Book of Mormon, for him, represented a confirmation of many archeological conclusions he had already determined. It became part of his academic library and was considered a book of value, but it did not cause in him any desire to change. His knowledge of the Book of Mormon was secular.

Pablo was an ignorant man, by all standards of the world. He was a simple laborer who had attended so little formal schooling that he was illiterate at the time we first taught him. With the help of his wife, he had completely mastered the content of the first one hundred pages of the Book of Mormon. He could recount with amazing accuracy the details of these pages. He had a love of the Book and considered it to be one of his most treasured possessions. His life was completely changed by what he had come to know. His knowledge of the Book of Mormon was divine.

For spiritual growth and fortification, we must know the things of God through the Holy Spirit. The temple has been referred to as the Lord's university. The knowledge gained through temple worship is learned through the Spirit and will effect change in the individual. This is how you can tell if the gospel knowledge you have gained is secular or divine. If the knowledge of sacred truths causes no change in your heart, no increased desire to repent and be obedient, then the knowledge is of the world. It is secular. Divine knowledge will always be associated with a desire to change, a desire to be better and more faithful in all things. The holy temple insures that a person has ready access to a sacred place where all learning is through the spirit and all knowledge received is divine. Within the walls of the temple, where the Spirit is ready to increase understanding and enlighten the mind, you continue to learn additional truth from both the narrative and visual symbolism. This deeper learning and more profound understanding could never come through searching a site on the Internet.

Amulek clearly knew the difference between knowing the things of God through secular learning and knowing the things of God through the Spirit. As recorded in the book of Alma, Amulek was, essentially, an inactive member of the Church. In these verses he first describes his linage back the Lehi. He makes it clear that he was a man of considerable riches and social standing. In a later verse he seems to contradict himself when he declares he had "never known much of the things of God." He then quickly recounts and says, "I mistake," and declares that he had seen the power of God in the preservation of his people. It is in the last verse where it becomes clear that Amulek knew that there existed two ways to know the truths of God. He declares, "I knew concerning these things, but I would not know; therefore I went on rebelling against God." Unless Amulek was talking about two different ways of knowing the things of God, this statement makes no sense. Consider his words,

> I am Amulek; I am the son of Giddonah, who was the son of Ishmael, who was a descendant of Aminadi; and it was the same Aminadi who interpreted the writing which was upon the wall of the temple, which was written by the finger of God.
>
> And Aminadi was a descendant of Nephi, who was the son of Lehi, who came out of the land of Jerusalem, who was a descendant of Manasseh, who was the son of Joseph who was sold into Egypt by the hands of his brethren.
>
> And behold, I am also a man of no small reputation among all those who know me; yea, and behold, I have many kindreds and friends, and I have also acquired much riches by the hand of my industry.
>
> Nevertheless, after all this, I never have known much of the ways of the Lord, and his mysteries and marvelous power. I said I never had known much of these things; but behold, I mistake, for I have seen much of his mysteries and his marvelous power; yea, even in the preservation of the lives of this people.
>
> Nevertheless, I did harden my heart, for I was called many times and I would not hear; therefore I knew concerning these things, yet I would not know; therefore I went on rebelling against God, in the wickedness of my heart, even until the fourth day of this seventh month, which is in the tenth year of the reign of the judges. (Alma 10:2–6)

Amulek had secular knowledge of God's "mysteries and his marvelous power," but he would not know them through the divine power of the Holy Spirit; therefore, in his own words, he "went on rebelling against God." Secular knowledge of the mysteries of heaven did not change his heart and did not bring him to Christ. All this changed as he began his association with Alma. He was changed forever once his knowledge of God came through the vehicle of the Spirit.

Christ also taught of these two ways to know Him when he asked his apostles the question, "But whom say ye that I am?"

> When Jesus came into the coasts of Caesarea Philippi, he asked his disciples, saying, Whom do men say that I the Son of man am?
> And they said, Some say that thou art John the Baptist: some, Elias; and others, Jeremias, or one of the prophets.
> He saith unto them, But whom say ye that I am?
> And Simon Peter answered and said, Thou art the Christ, the Son of the living God.
> And Jesus answered and said unto him, Blessed art thou, Simon Bar-jona: for flesh and blood hath not revealed it unto thee, but my Father which is in heaven. (Matthew 16:13–17)

The Lord knew that many of the superstitious people of his day had bizarre notions of who he was. What he really wanted to hear on this occasion was who his disciples believed him to be. Peter answered immediately, "Thou art the Christ, the Son of the Living God," and the Savior blessed him for his response. He blessed Peter because He knew Peter did not come to know this truth through the method of "flesh and blood," or in other words, through secular learning. "Flesh and blood hath not revealed it unto thee" is a clear declaration that there was an alternative way Peter could have known that Jesus was the Christ. This would be secular understanding or in Christ's words, flesh and blood understanding. He blessed Peter because he knew that his declaration came by revelation from "my Father which is in heaven."

If Peter's knowledge of the divinity of the Savior had been purely secular, he might have answered Christ's question like this:

"Well Lord, I have been with thee these almost three years. I have seen thy great miracles and I have listened to thy doctrine.

I have compared that which ye hath done and that which ye hath said to what was prophesied by our ancient prophets. I have given much thought and study to the matter and have debated the issue at some length with others. After all of this, I believe that Thou art the Christ, the Son of the Living God."

This would be pure secular knowledge of the Savior. If Peter had offered such a response, the Lord would never have blessed him. He might have responded instead, "Oh Peter, I fear for your soul, for flesh and blood hath revealed this unto you and not my Father which is in heaven"

Peter declared his testimony of Christ based on the personal and divine revelation he had received. He was blessed by the Savior because of this divine knowledge that would form the foundation upon which Peter would build a life of pure discipleship, a life that would be forever changed, and a life that he would ultimately forfeit for his personal conviction of the Savior.

In the case presented above, Blain questioned whether the temple had in some way been defiled by the actions of apostates. He was shocked that anyone with access to the Internet could obtain knowledge about the sacred ordinances of the temple. He was particularly bothered by the statement made by Brother Johns that there was "nothing he did not already know about the temple." There is, however, no risk whatsoever that Brother Johns, as an inactive member of the Church viewing the Internet, will ever know the great truths to be learned within a holy temple. Paul clearly teaches the reason for this when he declares that the natural man can never understand the things of God. He further teaches that God's truth can only be discerned spiritually.

> But the natural man receiveth not the things of the Spirit of God: for they are foolishness unto him: neither can he know them, because they are spiritually discerned. (1 Corinthians 2:14)

Paul makes it clear that Brother Johns cannot now receive or know the things of God. To him they can represent nothing more than a passing curiosity of something he would consider "foolishness." After viewing them he gains only the most superficial understanding of the content of the endowment, but all further learning is impossible without the Spirit of God. Without the temple, spiritual discernment of the sacred symbolism is impossible. Apostates may reveal the content of those holy ordinances, but they cannot impart the divine knowledge that is available to those who regularly enter the temple to bless those on the other side of the veil.

An apostate or nonmember will never be changed spiritually by the knowledge he might gain through an Internet site. Brother Ramirez, from the first missionary experience shared at the beginning of the chapter, gained an academic understanding of the Book of Mormon, but this knowledge brought no positive change into his life. The same would be true for anyone whose knowledge of the temple came through illicit means. The actions of apostates, in revealing that which they covenanted not to reveal, have nothing to do with the members of the Church. We have covenanted to keep these things sacred and not reveal them. We would, therefore, make no comment regarding the content of these Internet sites; we would not visit them or give any credibility to their content or purpose. The risk of casting "pearls before swine" is not that the pig will recognize the value of the pearl, but that he will simply trample it into the mud, completely ignorant of what he is doing (Matthew 7:6).

Therefore, the goal in this life is to gain divine knowledge of the things of God, to discern them spiritually. No physical place on earth offers a more inviting environment to learn truth through the Holy Spirit than God's temples.

Conclusion

The temple offers mankind a refuge from the world and from all that is or has been corrupted and distorted by the wisdom and foolishness of man. It offers a way to withdraw from the world for a short time and feel a very personal and real connection to that which is divine. It is where we learn how to be in the presence of God. All the truth that is learned in the temple comes through the Holy Spirit. No man will ever stand in the temple and expound truth for others to hear. The narrative is simple but offers deep and richly symbolic meaning that has the potential to teach all the knowledge of Godliness through silent meditation and learning. The degree to which a person comes to these deeper truths is dependent on his degree of personal righteousness and his faithfulness in coming to the temple with sufficient frequency to experience this higher order of learning.

Each member of the Church seeks a personal witness of Christ upon which a life of righteousness can be built. The temple is that sanctuary that guarantees all learning will come through the Spirit. Divine knowledge obtained through the Spirit helps us change from the natural man to a disciple of Christ.

There are many reasons we should go to the temple. We choose to go of our own choice, without being obligated or commanded. This emulates the free will offering of the Savior in Gethsemane and on the cross. We go to serve others without receiving recognition or thanks. Service given in this relatively anonymous way enriches our soul. The service we give in the temple involves doing for others what they cannot do for themselves. This too is a similitude of Christ doing for us, through His atoning sacrifice, what we could never do for ourselves. We go to the temple to seek peace, inspiration, and quiet reflection. There we can find answers to prayers, direction in how to help a child, a clearer vision of how to magnify our calling in the Church, and so much more. We go to the temple to bind families together forever. It allows us to leave the world for a few precious moments and be surrounded by that which is divine and celestial. Finally, we go to the temple to be taught and inspired through the process of silent learning, personal prayer, and quiet reflection.

All men and women in mortality need the blessings of the temple in their lives. Not just those blessings promised in our first visit when the endowment is received or when a sealing ordinance is performed, but the ongoing blessing of having the temple as a regular part of our worship of God and our personal spiritual nourishment. Come to the temple. Seek the guidance of the Holy Spirit to give direction to your life and understanding to your mind. There is no season of life when the temple will not bring these promised blessings.

ABOUT THE AUTHOR

Terrance Drake was born in Michigan in 1944. He was raised in Southern California and attended UCLA for three years prior to his mission to Mexico. After his mission, he married Marvia Lynn Brown in the Los Angeles Temple, and then he attended medical school in Michigan. They started their family immediately and had babies during medical school, during his internship, during his residency, and during his fellowship years.

Terrance specialized in OB/GYN and sub-specialized in Reproductive Endocrinology. He has six children and fourteen grandchildren, so far. Marvia and Terrance co-authored a book in 1984 called *Teaching Your Child about Sex*. Terrance has about thirty medical publications on infertility research, and he has been on the medical faculty of the Armed Forces Medical School in Bethesda, Sinai Medical Center in Baltimore, and the University of Nevada Medical School in Reno. He retired in 2000.

Terrance and Marvia served together in the Dominican Republic as temple workers. Terrance also served as the area doctor there. In Bolivia, he served as mission president, and in the Reno temple as first counselor and recorder. Terrance is a sealer and received the sealing power from Elder Oaks. Terrance and Marvia are currently serving in Peru, Terrance as area medical doctor and together as ordinance workers in the Lima Temple. Terrance is also serving in the presidency of the MTC in Lima. Other callings he has had in the Church include bishop, high councilor, young men president, seminary teacher, ward mission leader, and scoutmaster.

0 26575 53320 0